These field notes belong to:

____

If you accept my words and store up
my commands within you... and if you
look for it as for silver and search for
it as for hidden treasure, then you will
understand the fear of the LORD and
find the knowledge of God.

Proverbs 2:1,4–5

NIV

Adventure Bible

Field Notes

John

My First Bible Journal

Features written by
Lawrence O. Richards

ZONDERkidz

NIV Adventure Bible Field Notes, John
Published by Zondervan, 2021
Grand Rapids, Michigan, USA

www.Zondervan.com

This Bible was set in the Zondervan NIV Typeface, created at the 2K/DENMARK type foundry.

N120712

Contents

Preface to the New International Version

The goal of the New International Version (NIV) is to enable English-speaking people from around the world to read and hear God's eternal Word in their own language. Our work as translators is motivated by our conviction that the Bible is God's Word in written form. We believe that the Bible contains the divine answer to the deepest needs of humanity, sheds unique light on our path in a dark world and sets forth the way to our eternal well-being. Out of these deep convictions, we have sought to recreate as far as possible the experience of the original audience — blending transparency to the original text with accessibility for the millions of English speakers around the world. We have prioritized accuracy, clarity and literary quality with the goal of creating a translation suitable for public and private reading, evangelism, teaching, preaching, memorizing and liturgical use. We have also sought to preserve a measure of continuity with the long tradition of translating the Scriptures into English.

The complete NIV Bible was first published in 1978. It was a completely new translation made by over a hundred scholars working directly from the best available Hebrew, Aramaic and Greek texts. The translators came from the United States, Great Britain, Canada, Australia and New Zealand, giving the translation an international scope. They were from many denominations and churches — including Anglican, Assemblies of God, Baptist, Brethren, Christian Reformed, Church of Christ, Evangelical Covenant, Evangelical Free, Lutheran, Mennonite, Methodist, Nazarene, Presbyterian, Wesleyan and others. This breadth of denominational and theological perspective helped to safeguard the translation from sectarian bias. For these reasons, and by the grace of God, the NIV has gained a wide readership in all parts of the English-speaking world.

The work of translating the Bible is never finished. As good as they are, English translations must be regularly updated so that they will continue to communicate accurately the meaning of God's Word. Updates are needed in order to reflect the latest developments in our understanding of the biblical world and its languages and to keep pace with changes in English usage. Recognizing, then, that the NIV would retain its ability to communicate God's Word accurately only if it were regularly updated, the original translators established the Committee on Bible Translation (CBT). The Committee is a self-perpetuating group of biblical scholars charged with keeping abreast of advances in biblical scholarship and changes in English and issuing periodic updates to the NIV. The CBT is an independent, self-governing body and has sole responsibility for the NIV text. The Committee mirrors the original group of translators in its diverse international and denominational makeup and in its unifying commitment to the Bible as God's inspired Word.

In obedience to its mandate, the Committee has issued periodic updates to the NIV. An initial revision was released in 1984. A more thorough revision process was completed in 2005, resulting in the separately published TNIV. The updated NIV you now have in your hands builds on both the original NIV and the TNIV and represents the latest effort of the Committee to articulate God's unchanging Word in the way the original authors might have said it had they been speaking in English to the global English-speaking audience today.

Translation Philosophy

The Committee's translating work has been governed by three widely accepted principles about the way people use words and about the way we understand them.

First, the meaning of words is determined by the way that users of the language actually use them at any given time. For the biblical languages, therefore, the Committee utilizes the best and most recent scholarship on the way Hebrew, Aramaic and Greek words were being used in biblical times. At the same time, the Committee carefully studies the state of modern English. Good translation is like good communication: one must know the target audience so that the appropriate choices can be made about which English words to use to represent the original words of Scripture. From its inception, the NIV has had as its target the general English-speaking population all over the world, the "International" in its title reflecting this concern. The aim of the Committee is to put the Scriptures into natural English that will communicate effectively with the broadest possible audience of English speakers.

Modern technology has enhanced the Committee's ability to choose the right English words to convey the meaning of the original text. The field of computational linguistics harnesses the power of computers to provide broadly applicable and current data about the state of the language. Translators can now access huge databases of modern English to better understand the current meaning and usage of key words. The Committee utilized this resource in preparing the 2011 edition of the NIV. An area of especially rapid and significant change in English is the way certain nouns and pronouns are used to refer to human beings. The Committee therefore requested experts in computational linguistics at Collins Dictionaries to pose some key questions about this usage to its database of English — the largest in the world, with over 4.4 billion words, gathered from several English-speaking countries and including both spoken and written English. (The Collins Study, called "The Development and Use of Gender Language in Contemporary English," can be accessed at *http://www.thenivbible.com/about-the-niv/about-the-2011-edition/*.) The study revealed that the most popular words to describe the human race in modern U.S. English were "humanity," "man" and "mankind." The Committee then used this data in the updated NIV, choosing from among these three words (and occasionally others also) depending on the context.

A related issue creates a larger problem for modern translations: the move away from using the third-person masculine singular pronouns — "he/him/his" — to refer to men and women equally. This usage does persist in some forms of English, and this revision therefore occasionally uses these pronouns in a generic sense. But the tendency, recognized in day-to-day usage and confirmed by the Collins study, is away from the generic use of "he," "him" and "his." In recognition of this shift in language and in an effort to translate into the natural English that people are actually using, this revision of the NIV generally uses other constructions when the biblical text is plainly addressed to men and women equally. The reader will encounter especially frequently a "they," "their" or "them" to express a generic singular idea. Thus, for instance, Mark 8:36 reads: "What good is it for someone to gain the whole world, yet forfeit their soul?" This generic use of the "distributive" or "singular" "they/them/their" has been used for many centuries by respected writers of English and has now become established as standard English, spoken and written, all over the world.

A second linguistic principle that feeds into the Committee's translation work is that meaning is found not in individual words, as vital as they are, but in larger clusters: phrases, clauses, sentences, discourses. Translation is not, as many people think, a matter of word substitution: English word *x* in place of Hebrew word *y*. Translators must first determine the meaning of the words of the biblical languages in the context of the passage and then select English words that accurately communicate that meaning to modern listeners and readers. This means that accurate translation will not always reflect the exact structure of the original language. To be sure, there is debate over the degree to which translators should try to preserve the "form" of the original text in English. From the beginning, the NIV has taken a mediating position on this issue. The manual produced when the translation that became the NIV was first being planned states: "If the Greek or Hebrew syntax has a good parallel in modern English, it should be used. But if there is no good parallel, the English syntax appropriate to the meaning of the original is to be chosen." It is fine, in other words, to carry over the form of the biblical languages into English — but not at the expense of natural expression. The principle that meaning resides in larger clusters of words means that the Committee has not insisted on a "word-for-word" approach to translation. We certainly believe that every word of Scripture is inspired by God and therefore to be carefully studied to determine what God is saying to us. It is for this reason that the Committee labors over every single word of the original texts, working hard to determine how each of those words contributes to what the text is saying. Ultimately, however, it is how these individual words function in combination with other words that determines meaning.

A third linguistic principle guiding the Committee in its translation work is the recognition that words have a spectrum of meaning. It is popular to define a word by using another word, or "gloss," to substitute for it. This substitute word is then sometimes called the "literal" meaning of a word. In fact, however, words have a range of possible meanings. Those meanings will vary depending on the context, and words in one language will usually not occupy the same semantic range as words in another language. The Committee therefore studies each original word of Scripture in its context to identify its meaning in a particular verse and then chooses an appropriate English word (or phrase) to represent it. It is impossible, then, to translate any given Hebrew, Aramaic or Greek word with the same English word all the time. The Committee does try to translate related occurrences of a word in the original languages with the same English word in order to preserve the connection for the English reader. But the Committee generally privileges clear natural meaning over a concern with consistency in rendering particular words.

Textual Basis

For the Old Testament the standard Hebrew text, the Masoretic Text as published in the latest edition of *Biblia Hebraica*, has been used throughout. The Masoretic Text tradition contains marginal notations that offer variant readings. These have sometimes been followed instead of the text itself. Because such instances involve variants within the Masoretic tradition, they have not been indicated in the textual notes. In a few cases, words in the basic consonantal text have been divided differently than in the Masoretic Text. Such cases are usually indicated in the textual footnotes. The Dead Sea Scrolls contain biblical texts that represent an earlier stage of the transmission of the Hebrew text. They have been consulted, as have been the Samaritan Pentateuch and the ancient scribal traditions concerning deliberate textual changes. The translators also consulted the more important early versions. Readings from these versions, the Dead Sea Scrolls and the scribal traditions were occasionally followed where the Masoretic Text seemed doubtful and where accepted principles of textual criticism showed that one or more of these textual witnesses appeared to provide the correct reading. In rare cases, the translators have emended the Hebrew text where it appears to have become corrupted at an even earlier stage of its transmission. These departures from the Masoretic Text are also indicated in the textual footnotes. Sometimes the vowel indicators (which are later additions to the basic consonantal text) found in the Masoretic Text did not, in the judgment of the translators, represent the correct vowels for the original text. Accordingly, some words have been read with a different set of vowels. These instances are usually not indicated in the footnotes.

The Greek text used in translating the New Testament has been an eclectic one, based on the latest editions of the Nestle-Aland/United Bible Societies' Greek New Testament. The translators have made their choices among the variant readings in accordance with widely accepted principles of New Testament textual criticism. Footnotes call attention to places where uncertainty remains.

The New Testament authors, writing in Greek, often quote the Old Testament from its ancient Greek version, the Septuagint. This is one reason why some of the Old Testament quotations in the NIV New Testament are not identical to the corresponding passages in the NIV Old Testament. Such quotations in the New Testament are indicated with the footnote "(see Septuagint)."

Footnotes and Formatting

Footnotes in this version are of several kinds, most of which need no explanation. Those giving alternative translations begin with "Or" and generally introduce the alternative with the last word preceding it in the text, except when it is a single-word alternative. When poetry is quoted in a footnote a slash mark indicates a line division.

It should be noted that references to diseases, minerals, flora and fauna, architectural details, clothing, jewelry, musical instruments and other articles cannot always be identified with precision. Also, linear measurements and measures of capacity can only be approximated (see the Table of Weights and Measures). Although *Selah*, used mainly in the Psalms, is probably a musical term, its meaning is uncertain. Since it may interrupt reading and distract the reader, this word has not been kept in the English text, but every occurrence has been signaled by a footnote.

As an aid to the reader, sectional headings have been inserted. They are not to be regarded as part of the biblical text and are not intended for oral reading. It is the Committee's hope that these headings may prove more helpful to the reader than the traditional chapter divisions, which were introduced long after the Bible was written.

Sometimes the chapter and/or verse numbering in English translations of the Old Testament differs from that found in published Hebrew texts. This is particularly the case in the Psalms, where the traditional titles are included in the Hebrew verse numbering. Such differences are indicated in the footnotes at the bottom of the page. In the New Testament, verse numbers that marked off portions of the traditional English text not supported by the best Greek manuscripts now appear in brackets, with a footnote indicating the text that has been omitted (see, for example, Matthew 17:[21]).

Mark 16:9 – 20 and John 7:53 — 8:11, although long accorded virtually equal status with the rest of the Gospels in which they stand, have a questionable standing in the textual history of the New Testament, as noted in the bracketed annotations with which they are set off. A different typeface has been chosen for these passages to indicate their uncertain status.

Basic formatting of the text, such as lining the poetry, paragraphing (both prose and poetry), setting up of (administrative-like) lists, indenting letters and lengthy prayers within narratives and the insertion of sectional headings, has been the work of the Committee. However, the choice between single-column and double-column formats has been left to the publishers. Also the issuing of "red-letter" editions is a publisher's choice — one that the Committee does not endorse.

The Committee has again been reminded that every human effort is flawed — including this revision of the NIV. We trust, however, that many will find in it an improved representation of the Word of God, through which they hear his call to faith in our Lord Jesus Christ and to service in his kingdom. We offer this version of the Bible to him in whose name and for whose glory it has been made.

The Committee on Bible Translation

John

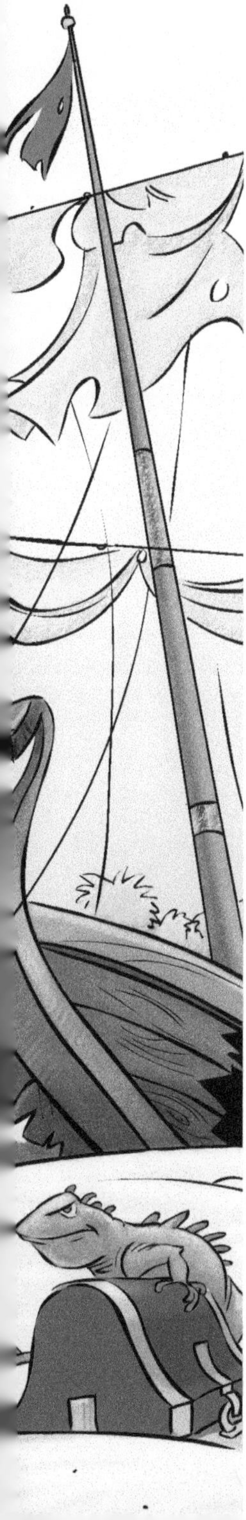

Who wrote this book?
John, the disciple of Jesus, wrote this book.

Why was this book written?
The Gospel of John shows that Jesus is the Son of God and helps people believe in him.

For whom was this book written?
John was written for everyone who wants to understand who Jesus really is.

What happens in this book?
John reports miracles and teachings that show that Jesus is the Son of God.

Who is the key person in this book?
Jesus is the most important person in this book.

When did this happen?
Jesus taught and performed miracles from AD 26 to 30.

Where did this happen?
Most of the events in this book happened in Judea.

What are some of the stories in this book?

Jesus chooses disciples	John 1:35–51
Jesus teaches Nicodemus	John 3:1–21
Jesus and a Samaritan woman	John 4:1–26
Jesus walks on water	John 6:16–24
Jesus says he is God's Son	John 8:31–59
Jesus heals a blind man	John 9:1–41
The good shepherd	John 10:1–21
Jesus raises Lazarus	John 11:1–44
Jesus rides into Jerusalem	John 12:12–19
Washing the disciples' feet	John 13:1–17
Praying for the disciples	John 17:6–19
Jesus is crucified	John 19:1–42
Jesus is raised to life	John 20:1–31
Jesus forgives Peter	John 21:15–25

The Word Became Flesh

1 In the beginning was the Word, and the Word was with God, and the Word was
God. 2 He was with God in the beginning. 3 Through him all things were made;
without him nothing was made that has been made. 4 In him was life, and that life
was the light of all mankind. 5 The light shines in the darkness, and the darkness
has not overcome[a] it.
6 There was a man sent from God whose name was John. 7 He came as a witness
to testify concerning that light, so that through him all might believe. 8 He himself
was not the light; he came only as a witness to the light.
9 The true light that gives light to everyone was coming into the world. 10 He was
in the world, and though the world was made through him, the world did not rec-
ognize him. 11 He came to that which was his own, but his own did not receive him.
12 Yet to all who did receive him, to those who believed in his name, he gave the right
to become children of God — 13 children born not of natural descent, nor of human
decision or a husband's will, but born of God.
14 The Word became flesh and made his dwelling among us. We have seen his
glory, the glory of the one and only Son, who came from the Father, full of grace
and truth.
15 (John testified concerning him. He cried out, saying, "This is the one I spoke
about when I said, 'He who comes after me has surpassed me because he was be-
fore me.'") 16 Out of his fullness we have all received grace in place of grace already
given. 17 For the law was given through Moses; grace and truth came through Jesus
Christ. 18 No one has ever seen God, but the one and only Son, who is himself God
and[b] is in closest relationship with the Father, has made him known.

John the Baptist Denies Being the Messiah

19 Now this was John's testimony when the Jewish leaders[c] in Jerusalem sent
priests and Levites to ask him who he was. 20 He did not fail to confess, but con-
fessed freely, "I am not the Messiah."
21 They asked him, "Then who are you? Are you Elijah?"
He said, "I am not."
"Are you the Prophet?"
He answered, "No."
22 Finally they said, "Who are you? Give us an answer to take back to those who
sent us. What do you say about yourself?"
23 John replied in the words of Isaiah the prophet, "I am the voice of one calling
in the wilderness, 'Make straight the way for the Lord.'"[d]
24 Now the Pharisees who had been sent 25 questioned him, "Why then do you
baptize if you are not the Messiah, nor Elijah, nor the Prophet?"
26 "I baptize with[e] water," John replied, "but among you stands one you do not
know. 27 He is the one who comes after me, the straps of whose sandals I am not
worthy to untie."
28 This all happened at Bethany on the other side of the Jordan, where John was
baptizing.

[a] *5* Or *understood* [b] *18* Some manuscripts *but the only Son, who* [c] *19* The Greek term traditionally translated *the Jews* (*hoi Ioudaioi*) refers here and elsewhere in John's Gospel to those Jewish leaders who opposed Jesus; also in 5:10, 15, 16; 7:1, 11, 13; 9:22; 18:14, 28, 36; 19:7, 12, 31, 38; 20:19. [d] *23* Isaiah 40:3 [e] *26* Or *in*; also in verses 31 and 33 (twice)

John Testifies About Jesus

29The next day John saw Jesus coming toward him and said, "Look, the Lamb of
God, who takes away the sin of the world! 30This is the one I meant when I said, 'A
man who comes after me has surpassed me because he was before me.' 31I myself
did not know him, but the reason I came baptizing with water was that he might
be revealed to Israel."

32Then John gave this testimony: "I saw the Spirit come down from heaven as a
dove and remain on him. 33And I myself did not know him, but the one who sent me
to baptize with water told me, 'The man on whom you see the Spirit come down
and remain is the one who will baptize with the Holy Spirit.' 34I have seen and I tes-
tify that this is God's Chosen One."[a]

John's Disciples Follow Jesus

35The next day John was there again with two of his disciples. 36When he saw
Jesus passing by, he said, "Look, the Lamb of God!"

37When the two disciples heard him say this, they followed Jesus. 38Turning
around, Jesus saw them following and asked, "What do you want?"

They said, "Rabbi" (which means "Teacher"), "where are you staying?"

39"Come," he replied, "and you will see."

So they went and saw where he was staying, and they spent that day with him.
It was about four in the afternoon.

40Andrew, Simon Peter's brother, was one of the two who heard what John had
said and who had followed Jesus. 41The first thing Andrew did was to find his broth-
er Simon and tell him, "We have found the Messiah" (that is, the Christ). 42And he
brought him to Jesus.

Jesus looked at him and said, "You are Simon son of John. You will be called Ce-
phas" (which, when translated, is Peter[b]).

Jesus Calls Philip and Nathanael

43The next day Jesus decided to leave for Galilee. Finding Philip, he said to him,
"Follow me."

44Philip, like Andrew and Peter, was from the town of Bethsaida. 45Philip found
Nathanael and told him, "We have found the one Moses wrote about in the Law,
and about whom the prophets also wrote — Jesus of Nazareth, the son of Joseph."

46"Nazareth! Can anything good come from there?" Nathanael asked.

"Come and see," said Philip.

47When Jesus saw Nathanael approaching, he said of him, "Here truly is an Isra-
elite in whom there is no deceit."

48"How do you know me?" Nathanael asked.

Jesus answered, "I saw you while you were still under the fig tree before Philip
called you."

49Then Nathanael declared, "Rabbi, you are the Son of God; you are the king of Israel."

50Jesus said, "You believe[c] because I told you I saw you under the fig tree. You will
see greater things than that." 51He then added, "Very truly I tell you,[d] you[d] will see
'heaven open, and the angels of God ascending and descending on'[e] the Son of Man."

[a] *34* See Isaiah 42:1; many manuscripts *is the Son of God.* [b] *42* *Cephas* (Aramaic) and *Peter* (Greek) both mean *rock.* [c] *50* Or *Do you believe . . . ?* [d] *51* The Greek is plural. [e] *51* Gen. 28:12

Jesus Changes Water Into Wine

2 On the third day a wedding took place at Cana in Galilee. Jesus' mother was
there, 2and Jesus and his disciples had also been invited to the wedding. 3When
the wine was gone, Jesus' mother said to him, "They have no more wine."
4"Woman,[a] why do you involve me?" Jesus replied. "My hour has not yet come."
5His mother said to the servants, "Do whatever he tells you."
6Nearby stood six stone water jars, the kind used by the Jews for ceremonial
washing, each holding from twenty to thirty gallons.[b]
7Jesus said to the servants, "Fill the jars with water"; so they filled them to the
brim.
8Then he told them, "Now draw some out and take it to the master of the banquet."
They did so, 9and the master of the banquet tasted the water that had been
turned into wine. He did not realize where it had come from, though the servants who had drawn the water knew. Then he called the bridegroom aside
10and said, "Everyone brings out the choice wine first and then the cheaper
wine after the guests have had too much to drink; but you have saved the best
till now."
11What Jesus did here in Cana of Galilee was the first of the signs through which
he revealed his glory; and his disciples believed in him.
12After this he went down to Capernaum with his mother and brothers and his
disciples. There they stayed for a few days.

Jesus Clears the Temple Courts

13When it was almost time for the Jewish Passover, Jesus went up to Jerusalem. 14In the temple courts he found people selling cattle, sheep and doves, and
others sitting at tables exchanging money. 15So he made a whip out of cords,
and drove all from the temple courts, both sheep and cattle; he scattered the
coins of the money changers and overturned their tables. 16To those who sold
doves he said, "Get these out of here! Stop turning my Father's house into a
market!" 17His disciples remembered that it is written: "Zeal for your house will
consume me."[c]
18The Jews then responded to him, "What sign can you show us to prove your
authority to do all this?"
19Jesus answered them, "Destroy this temple, and I will raise it again in three
days."
20They replied, "It has taken forty-six years to build this temple, and you are
going to raise it in three days?" 21But the temple he had spoken of was his body.
22After he was raised from the dead, his disciples recalled what he had said. Then
they believed the scripture and the words that Jesus had spoken.
23Now while he was in Jerusalem at the Passover Festival, many people saw the
signs he was performing and believed in his name.[d] 24But Jesus would not entrust
himself to them, for he knew all people. 25He did not need any testimony about
mankind, for he knew what was in each person.

[a] *4* The Greek for *Woman* does not denote any disrespect. [b] *6* Or from about 75 to about 115 liters
[c] *17* Psalm 69:9 [d] *23* Or *in him*

Life in Bible Times

Water Jars

Water was stored in large stone jars and was used for washing and drinking. Jews at the time of Jesus did much ceremonial washing of their hands before eating. These very large jars were the same kind that Jesus asked to have filled with water before he changed that water to wine.

Jesus Teaches Nicodemus

3 Now there was a Pharisee, a man named Nicodemus who was a member of the
Jewish ruling council. 2He came to Jesus at night and said, "Rabbi, we know
that you are a teacher who has come from God. For no one could perform the signs
you are doing if God were not with him."
3Jesus replied, "Very truly I tell you, no one can see the kingdom of God unless
they are born again.[a]"
4"How can someone be born when they are old?" Nicodemus asked. "Surely they
cannot enter a second time into their mother's womb to be born!"
5Jesus answered, "Very truly I tell you, no one can enter the kingdom of God un-
less they are born of water and the Spirit. 6Flesh gives birth to flesh, but the Spirit[b]
gives birth to spirit. 7You should not be surprised at my saying, 'You[c] must be born
again.' 8The wind blows wherever it pleases. You hear its sound, but you cannot tell
where it comes from or where it is going. So it is with everyone born of the Spirit."[d]
9"How can this be?" Nicodemus asked.
10"You are Israel's teacher," said Jesus, "and do you not understand these things?
11Very truly I tell you, we speak of what we know, and we testify to what we have
seen, but still you people do not accept our testimony. 12I have spoken to you of
earthly things and you do not believe; how then will you believe if I speak of heav-
enly things? 13No one has ever gone into heaven except the one who came from
heaven — the Son of Man.[e] 14Just as Moses lifted up the snake in the wilderness, so
the Son of Man must be lifted up,[f] 15that everyone who believes may have eternal
life in him."[g]
16For God so loved the world that he gave his one and only Son, that whoev-
er believes in him shall not perish but have eternal life. 17For God did not send
his Son into the world to condemn the world, but to save the world through
him. 18Whoever believes in him is not condemned, but whoever does not be-
lieve stands condemned already because they have not believed in the name of
God's one and only Son. 19This is the verdict: Light has come into the world, but
people loved darkness instead of light because their deeds were evil. 20Every-
one who does evil hates the light, and will not come into the light for fear that
their deeds will be exposed. 21But whoever lives by the truth comes into the
light, so that it may be seen plainly that what they have done has been done
in the sight of God.

John Testifies Again About Jesus

22After this, Jesus and his disciples went out into the Judean countryside, where
he spent some time with them, and baptized. 23Now John also was baptizing at
Aenon near Salim, because there was plenty of water, and people were coming
and being baptized. 24(This was before John was put in prison.) 25An argument de-
veloped between some of John's disciples and a certain Jew over the matter of
ceremonial washing. 26They came to John and said to him, "Rabbi, that man who
was with you on the other side of the Jordan — the one you testified about — look,
he is baptizing, and everyone is going to him."

[a] *3* The Greek for *again* also means *from above*; also in verse 7. [b] *6* Or *but spirit* [c] *7* The Greek is plural. [d] *8* The Greek for *Spirit* is the same as that for *wind*. [e] *13* Some manuscripts *Man, who is in heaven* [f] *14* The Greek for *lifted up* also means *exalted*. [g] *15* Some interpreters end the quotation with verse 21.

Live It!

Born Again

Read John 3:1–16. When you were born, you received physical life. People who are "born again" receive eternal life from God. Physical life ends when people die, but a person with eternal life will live forever with God in heaven.

In the journal space below, write how you can know that you have been born again. Memorize John 3:16. If you believe in Jesus as your Savior, this verse says that you are born again and have eternal life.

John 3:1-16

27 To this John replied, "A person can receive only what is given them from heaven.
28 You yourselves can testify that I said, 'I am not the Messiah but am sent ahead
of him.' 29 The bride belongs to the bridegroom. The friend who attends the bride-
groom waits and listens for him, and is full of joy when he hears the bridegroom's
voice. That joy is mine, and it is now complete. 30 He must become greater; I must
become less."[a]
31 The one who comes from above is above all; the one who is from the earth
belongs to the earth, and speaks as one from the earth. The one who comes from
heaven is above all. 32 He testifies to what he has seen and heard, but no one ac-
cepts his testimony. 33 Whoever has accepted it has certified that God is truthful.
34 For the one whom God has sent speaks the words of God, for God[b] gives the Spirit
without limit. 35 The Father loves the Son and has placed everything in his hands.
36 Whoever believes in the Son has eternal life, but whoever rejects the Son will not
see life, for God's wrath remains on them.

Jesus Talks With a Samaritan Woman

4 Now Jesus learned that the Pharisees had heard that he was gaining and bap-
tizing more disciples than John — 2 although in fact it was not Jesus who bap-
tized, but his disciples. 3 So he left Judea and went back once more to Galilee.
4 Now he had to go through Samaria. 5 So he came to a town in Samaria called
Sychar, near the plot of ground Jacob had given to his son Joseph. 6 Jacob's well
was there, and Jesus, tired as he was from the journey, sat down by the well. It was
about noon.
7 When a Samaritan woman came to draw water, Jesus said to her, "Will you give
me a drink?" 8 (His disciples had gone into the town to buy food.)
9 The Samaritan woman said to him, "You are a Jew and I am a Samaritan wom-
an. How can you ask me for a drink?" (For Jews do not associate with Samaritans.[c])
10 Jesus answered her, "If you knew the gift of God and who it is that asks you
for a drink, you would have asked him and he would have given you living water."
11 "Sir," the woman said, "you have nothing to draw with and the well is deep.
Where can you get this living water? 12 Are you greater than our father Jacob, who
gave us the well and drank from it himself, as did also his sons and his livestock?"
13 Jesus answered, "Everyone who drinks this water will be thirsty again, 14 but
whoever drinks the water I give them will never thirst. Indeed, the water I give them
will become in them a spring of water welling up to eternal life."
15 The woman said to him, "Sir, give me this water so that I won't get thirsty and
have to keep coming here to draw water."
16 He told her, "Go, call your husband and come back."
17 "I have no husband," she replied.
Jesus said to her, "You are right when you say you have no husband. 18 The fact is,
you have had five husbands, and the man you now have is not your husband. What
you have just said is quite true."
19 "Sir," the woman said, "I can see that you are a prophet. 20 Our ancestors wor-
shiped on this mountain, but you Jews claim that the place where we must worship
is in Jerusalem."

[a] *30* Some interpreters end the quotation with verse 36. [b] *34* Greek *he* [c] *9* Or *do not use dishes Samaritans have used*

Life in Bible Times

Carrying Water

Getting each day's water supply was the job of the women in a town. Each day, morning and evening, they came to the town well, filled their jars, and then carried the full water jars home on their heads. The Samaritan woman in the story in John 4 probably came to the well at noon to avoid the other women of the community, who disapproved of her lifestyle.

21"Woman," Jesus replied, "believe me, a time is coming when you will worship
the Father neither on this mountain nor in Jerusalem. 22You Samaritans worship
what you do not know; we worship what we do know, for salvation is from the Jews.
23Yet a time is coming and has now come when the true worshipers will worship
the Father in the Spirit and in truth, for they are the kind of worshipers the Father
seeks. 24God is spirit, and his worshipers must worship in the Spirit and in truth."
25The woman said, "I know that Messiah" (called Christ) "is coming. When he
comes, he will explain everything to us."
26Then Jesus declared, "I, the one speaking to you — I am he."

The Disciples Rejoin Jesus

27Just then his disciples returned and were surprised to find him talking with a
woman. But no one asked, "What do you want?" or "Why are you talking with her?"
28Then, leaving her water jar, the woman went back to the town and said to the
people, 29"Come, see a man who told me everything I ever did. Could this be the
Messiah?" 30They came out of the town and made their way toward him.
31Meanwhile his disciples urged him, "Rabbi, eat something."
32But he said to them, "I have food to eat that you know nothing about."
33Then his disciples said to each other, "Could someone have brought him food?"
34"My food," said Jesus, "is to do the will of him who sent me and to finish his
work. 35Don't you have a saying, 'It's still four months until harvest'? I tell you, open
your eyes and look at the fields! They are ripe for harvest. 36Even now the one who
reaps draws a wage and harvests a crop for eternal life, so that the sower and the
reaper may be glad together. 37Thus the saying 'One sows and another reaps' is
true. 38I sent you to reap what you have not worked for. Others have done the hard
work, and you have reaped the benefits of their labor."

Many Samaritans Believe

39Many of the Samaritans from that town believed in him because of the wom-
an's testimony, "He told me everything I ever did." 40So when the Samaritans came
to him, they urged him to stay with them, and he stayed two days. 41And because
of his words many more became believers.
42They said to the woman, "We no longer believe just because of what you said;
now we have heard for ourselves, and we know that this man really is the Savior
of the world."

Jesus Heals an Official's Son

43After the two days he left for Galilee. 44(Now Jesus himself had pointed out
that a prophet has no honor in his own country.) 45When he arrived in Galilee, the
Galileans welcomed him. They had seen all that he had done in Jerusalem at the
Passover Festival, for they also had been there.
46Once more he visited Cana in Galilee, where he had turned the water into wine.
And there was a certain royal official whose son lay sick at Capernaum. 47When
this man heard that Jesus had arrived in Galilee from Judea, he went to him and
begged him to come and heal his son, who was close to death.
48"Unless you people see signs and wonders," Jesus told him, "you will never
believe."
49The royal official said, "Sir, come down before my child dies."
50"Go," Jesus replied, "your son will live."

The man took Jesus at his word and departed. 51While he was still on the way, his
servants met him with the news that his boy was living. 52When he inquired as to th
time when his son got better, they said to him, "Yesterday, at one in the afternoo
the fever left him."
53Then the father realized that this was the exact time at which Jesus had said t
him, "Your son will live." So he and his whole household believed.
54This was the second sign Jesus performed after coming from Judea to Galilee.

The Healing at the Pool

5 Some time later, Jesus went up to Jerusalem for one of the Jewish festivals.
2Now there is in Jerusalem near the Sheep Gate a pool, which in Aramaic is
called Bethesda[a] and which is surrounded by five covered colonnades. 3Here a great
number of disabled people used to lie — the blind, the lame, the paralyzed. [4][b] 5One
who was there had been an invalid for thirty-eight years. 6When Jesus saw him ly-
ing there and learned that he had been in this condition for a long time, he asked
him, "Do you want to get well?"
7"Sir," the invalid replied, "I have no one to help me into the pool when the water
is stirred. While I am trying to get in, someone else goes down ahead of me."
8Then Jesus said to him, "Get up! Pick up your mat and walk." 9At once the man
was cured; he picked up his mat and walked.
The day on which this took place was a Sabbath, 10and so the Jewish leaders
said to the man who had been healed, "It is the Sabbath; the law forbids you to
carry your mat."
11But he replied, "The man who made me well said to me, 'Pick up your mat and
walk.' "
12So they asked him, "Who is this fellow who told you to pick it up and walk?"
13The man who was healed had no idea who it was, for Jesus had slipped away
into the crowd that was there.
14Later Jesus found him at the temple and said to him, "See, you are well again.
Stop sinning or something worse may happen to you." 15The man went away and
told the Jewish leaders that it was Jesus who had made him well.

The Authority of the Son

16So, because Jesus was doing these things on the Sabbath, the Jewish leaders
began to persecute him. 17In his defense Jesus said to them, "My Father is always
at his work to this very day, and I too am working." 18For this reason they tried all
the more to kill him; not only was he breaking the Sabbath, but he was even calling
God his own Father, making himself equal with God.
19Jesus gave them this answer: "Very truly I tell you, the Son can do nothing by
himself; he can do only what he sees his Father doing, because whatever the Fa-
ther does the Son also does. 20For the Father loves the Son and shows him all he
does. Yes, and he will show him even greater works than these, so that you will be
amazed. 21For just as the Father raises the dead and gives them life, even so the
Son gives life to whom he is pleased to give it. 22Moreover, the Father judges no

[a] *2* Some manuscripts *Bethzatha*; other manuscripts *Bethsaida* [b] *3,4* Some manuscripts include here, wholly or in part, *paralyzed — and they waited for the moving of the waters.* *4From time to time an angel of the Lord would come down and stir up the waters. The first one into the pool after each such disturbance would be cured of whatever disease they had.*

one, but has entrusted all judgment to the Son, 23that all may honor the Son just as
they honor the Father. Whoever does not honor the Son does not honor the Father,
who sent him.

24"Very truly I tell you, whoever hears my word and believes him who sent me has
eternal life and will not be judged but has crossed over from death to life. 25Very
truly I tell you, a time is coming and has now come when the dead will hear the
voice of the Son of God and those who hear will live. 26For as the Father has life in
himself, so he has granted the Son also to have life in himself. 27And he has given
him authority to judge because he is the Son of Man.

28"Do not be amazed at this, for a time is coming when all who are in their graves
will hear his voice 29and come out — those who have done what is good will rise to
live, and those who have done what is evil will rise to be condemned. 30By myself
I can do nothing; I judge only as I hear, and my judgment is just, for I seek not to
please myself but him who sent me.

Testimonies About Jesus

31"If I testify about myself, my testimony is not true. 32There is another who testi-
fies in my favor, and I know that his testimony about me is true.

33"You have sent to John and he has testified to the truth. 34Not that I accept
human testimony; but I mention it that you may be saved. 35John was a lamp that
burned and gave light, and you chose for a time to enjoy his light.

36"I have testimony weightier than that of John. For the works that the Father has
given me to finish — the very works that I am doing — testify that the Father has
sent me. 37And the Father who sent me has himself testified concerning me. You
have never heard his voice nor seen his form, 38nor does his word dwell in you, for
you do not believe the one he sent. 39You study[a] the Scriptures diligently because
you think that in them you have eternal life. These are the very Scriptures that tes-
tify about me, 40yet you refuse to come to me to have life.

41"I do not accept glory from human beings, 42but I know you. I know that you do
not have the love of God in your hearts. 43I have come in my Father's name, and you
do not accept me; but if someone else comes in his own name, you will accept him.
44How can you believe since you accept glory from one another but do not seek the
glory that comes from the only God[b]?

45"But do not think I will accuse you before the Father. Your accuser is Moses, on
whom your hopes are set. 46If you believed Moses, you would believe me, for he
wrote about me. 47But since you do not believe what he wrote, how are you going
to believe what I say?"

Jesus Feeds the Five Thousand

6 Some time after this, Jesus crossed to the far shore of the Sea of Galilee (that is,
the Sea of Tiberias), 2and a great crowd of people followed him because they
saw the signs he had performed by healing the sick. 3Then Jesus went up on a moun-
tainside and sat down with his disciples. 4The Jewish Passover Festival was near.

5When Jesus looked up and saw a great crowd coming toward him, he said to
Philip, "Where shall we buy bread for these people to eat?" 6He asked this only to
test him, for he already had in mind what he was going to do.

[a] *39* Or *39Study* [b] *44* Some early manuscripts *the Only One*

Life in Bible Times

Barley Loaves

Two kinds of grain, wheat and barley, were used to make bread. Wheat was expensive. Most people were poor, so they ate small round loaves of coarse barley bread. The little boy in the story in John 6 had five of these loaves.

[7]Philip answered him, "It would take more than half a year's wages[a] to buy
enough bread for each one to have a bite!"
[8]Another of his disciples, Andrew, Simon Peter's brother, spoke up, [9]"Here is a boy
with five small barley loaves and two small fish, but how far will they go among
so many?"
[10]Jesus said, "Have the people sit down." There was plenty of grass in that place,
and they sat down (about five thousand men were there). [11]Jesus then took the
loaves, gave thanks, and distributed to those who were seated as much as they
wanted. He did the same with the fish.
[12]When they had all had enough to eat, he said to his disciples, "Gather the pieces
that are left over. Let nothing be wasted." [13]So they gathered them and filled twelve
baskets with the pieces of the five barley loaves left over by those who had eaten.
[14]After the people saw the sign Jesus performed, they began to say, "Surely this
is the Prophet who is to come into the world." [15]Jesus, knowing that they intended
to come and make him king by force, withdrew again to a mountain by himself.

Jesus Walks on the Water

[16]When evening came, his disciples went down to the lake, [17]where they got into
a boat and set off across the lake for Capernaum. By now it was dark, and Jesus
had not yet joined them. [18]A strong wind was blowing and the waters grew rough.
[19]When they had rowed about three or four miles,[b] they saw Jesus approaching the
boat, walking on the water; and they were frightened. [20]But he said to them, "It is
I; don't be afraid." [21]Then they were willing to take him into the boat, and immedi-
ately the boat reached the shore where they were heading.
[22]The next day the crowd that had stayed on the opposite shore of the lake re-
alized that only one boat had been there, and that Jesus had not entered it with
his disciples, but that they had gone away alone. [23]Then some boats from Tiberias
landed near the place where the people had eaten the bread after the Lord had giv-
en thanks. [24]Once the crowd realized that neither Jesus nor his disciples were there,
they got into the boats and went to Capernaum in search of Jesus.

Jesus the Bread of Life

[25]When they found him on the other side of the lake, they asked him, "Rabbi,
when did you get here?"
[26]Jesus answered, "Very truly I tell you, you are looking for me, not because you
saw the signs I performed but because you ate the loaves and had your fill. [27]Do not
work for food that spoils, but for food that endures to eternal life, which the Son
of Man will give you. For on him God the Father has placed his seal of approval."
[28]Then they asked him, "What must we do to do the works God requires?"
[29]Jesus answered, "The work of God is this: to believe in the one he has sent."
[30]So they asked him, "What sign then will you give that we may see it and be-
lieve you? What will you do? [31]Our ancestors ate the manna in the wilderness; as it
is written: 'He gave them bread from heaven to eat.'[c]"
[32]Jesus said to them, "Very truly I tell you, it is not Moses who has given you the
bread from heaven, but it is my Father who gives you the true bread from heaven.
[33]For the bread of God is the bread that comes down from heaven and gives life to
the world."

[a] *7* Greek *take two hundred denarii* [b] *19* Or about 5 or 6 kilometers [c] *31* Exodus 16:4; Neh. 9:15; Psalm 78:24,25

34“Sir,” they said, “always give us this bread.”
35Then Jesus declared, “I am the bread of life. Whoever comes to me will never
go hungry, and whoever believes in me will never be thirsty. 36But as I told you, you
have seen me and still you do not believe. 37All those the Father gives me will come
to me, and whoever comes to me I will never drive away. 38For I have come down
from heaven not to do my will but to do the will of him who sent me. 39And this is the
will of him who sent me, that I shall lose none of all those he has given me, but raise
them up at the last day. 40For my Father’s will is that everyone who looks to the Son
and believes in him shall have eternal life, and I will raise them up at the last day.”
41At this the Jews there began to grumble about him because he said, “I am the
bread that came down from heaven.” 42They said, “Is this not Jesus, the son of Jo-
seph, whose father and mother we know? How can he now say, ‘I came down from
heaven’?”
43“Stop grumbling among yourselves,” Jesus answered. 44“No one can come to
me unless the Father who sent me draws them, and I will raise them up at the last
day. 45It is written in the Prophets: ‘They will all be taught by God.’[a] Everyone who
has heard the Father and learned from him comes to me. 46No one has seen the
Father except the one who is from God; only he has seen the Father. 47Very truly I tell
you, the one who believes has eternal life. 48I am the bread of life. 49Your ancestors
ate the manna in the wilderness, yet they died. 50But here is the bread that comes
down from heaven, which anyone may eat and not die. 51I am the living bread that
came down from heaven. Whoever eats this bread will live forever. This bread is my
flesh, which I will give for the life of the world.”
52Then the Jews began to argue sharply among themselves, “How can this man
give us his flesh to eat?”
53Jesus said to them, “Very truly I tell you, unless you eat the flesh of the Son
of Man and drink his blood, you have no life in you. 54Whoever eats my flesh and
drinks my blood has eternal life, and I will raise them up at the last day. 55For my
flesh is real food and my blood is real drink. 56Whoever eats my flesh and drinks
my blood remains in me, and I in them. 57Just as the living Father sent me and I live
because of the Father, so the one who feeds on me will live because of me. 58This is
the bread that came down from heaven. Your ancestors ate manna and died, but
whoever feeds on this bread will live forever.” 59He said this while teaching in the
synagogue in Capernaum.

Many Disciples Desert Jesus

60On hearing it, many of his disciples said, “This is a hard teaching. Who can
accept it?”
61Aware that his disciples were grumbling about this, Jesus said to them, “Does
this offend you? 62Then what if you see the Son of Man ascend to where he was be-
fore! 63The Spirit gives life; the flesh counts for nothing. The words I have spoken
to you — they are full of the Spirit[b] and life. 64Yet there are some of you who do not
believe.” For Jesus had known from the beginning which of them did not believe
and who would betray him. 65He went on to say, “This is why I told you that no one
can come to me unless the Father has enabled them.”
66From this time many of his disciples turned back and no longer followed him.
67“You do not want to leave too, do you?” Jesus asked the Twelve.

[a] *45* Isaiah 54:13 [b] *63* Or are *Spirit*; or are *spirit*

68Simon Peter answered him, "Lord, to whom shall we go? You have the words
of eternal life. 69We have come to believe and to know that you are the Holy One
of God."
70Then Jesus replied, "Have I not chosen you, the Twelve? Yet one of you is a dev-
il!" 71(He meant Judas, the son of Simon Iscariot, who, though one of the Twelve,
was later to betray him.)

Jesus Goes to the Festival of Tabernacles

7 After this, Jesus went around in Galilee. He did not want[a] to go about in Judea
because the Jewish leaders there were looking for a way to kill him. 2But when
the Jewish Festival of Tabernacles was near, 3Jesus' brothers said to him, "Leave
Galilee and go to Judea, so that your disciples there may see the works you do.
4No one who wants to become a public figure acts in secret. Since you are doing
these things, show yourself to the world." 5For even his own brothers did not believe
in him.
6Therefore Jesus told them, "My time is not yet here; for you any time will do.
7The world cannot hate you, but it hates me because I testify that its works are evil.
8You go to the festival. I am not[b] going up to this festival, because my time has not
yet fully come." 9After he had said this, he stayed in Galilee.
10However, after his brothers had left for the festival, he went also, not publicly,
but in secret. 11Now at the festival the Jewish leaders were watching for Jesus and
asking, "Where is he?"
12Among the crowds there was widespread whispering about him. Some said,
"He is a good man."
Others replied, "No, he deceives the people." 13But no one would say anything
publicly about him for fear of the leaders.

Jesus Teaches at the Festival

14Not until halfway through the festival did Jesus go up to the temple courts and
begin to teach. 15The Jews there were amazed and asked, "How did this man get
such learning without having been taught?"
16Jesus answered, "My teaching is not my own. It comes from the one who
sent me. 17Anyone who chooses to do the will of God will find out whether my
teaching comes from God or whether I speak on my own. 18Whoever speaks
on their own does so to gain personal glory, but he who seeks the glory of the
one who sent him is a man of truth; there is nothing false about him. 19Has not
Moses given you the law? Yet not one of you keeps the law. Why are you trying
to kill me?"
20"You are demon-possessed," the crowd answered. "Who is trying to kill you?"
21Jesus said to them, "I did one miracle, and you are all amazed. 22Yet, because
Moses gave you circumcision (though actually it did not come from Moses, but
from the patriarchs), you circumcise a boy on the Sabbath. 23Now if a boy can be
circumcised on the Sabbath so that the law of Moses may not be broken, why are
you angry with me for healing a man's whole body on the Sabbath? 24Stop judging
by mere appearances, but instead judge correctly."

[a] *1* Some manuscripts *not have authority* [b] *8* Some manuscripts *not yet*

Division Over Who Jesus Is

25At that point some of the people of Jerusalem began to ask, "Isn't this the man
they are trying to kill? 26Here he is, speaking publicly, and they are not saying a
word to him. Have the authorities really concluded that he is the Messiah? 27But we
know where this man is from; when the Messiah comes, no one will know where
he is from."

28Then Jesus, still teaching in the temple courts, cried out, "Yes, you know me,
and you know where I am from. I am not here on my own authority, but he who
sent me is true. You do not know him, 29but I know him because I am from him and
he sent me."

30At this they tried to seize him, but no one laid a hand on him, because his hour
had not yet come. 31Still, many in the crowd believed in him. They said, "When the
Messiah comes, will he perform more signs than this man?"

32The Pharisees heard the crowd whispering such things about him. Then the
chief priests and the Pharisees sent temple guards to arrest him.

33Jesus said, "I am with you for only a short time, and then I am going to the one
who sent me. 34You will look for me, but you will not find me; and where I am, you
cannot come."

35The Jews said to one another, "Where does this man intend to go that we can-
not find him? Will he go where our people live scattered among the Greeks, and
teach the Greeks? 36What did he mean when he said, 'You will look for me, but you
will not find me,' and 'Where I am, you cannot come'?"

37On the last and greatest day of the festival, Jesus stood and said in a loud
voice, "Let anyone who is thirsty come to me and drink. 38Whoever believes in me,
as Scripture has said, rivers of living water will flow from within them."[a] 39By this he
meant the Spirit, whom those who believed in him were later to receive. Up to that
time the Spirit had not been given, since Jesus had not yet been glorified.

40On hearing his words, some of the people said, "Surely this man is the Prophet."

41Others said, "He is the Messiah."

Still others asked, "How can the Messiah come from Galilee? 42Does not Scripture
say that the Messiah will come from David's descendants and from Bethlehem, the
town where David lived?" 43Thus the people were divided because of Jesus. 44Some
wanted to seize him, but no one laid a hand on him.

Unbelief of the Jewish Leaders

45Finally the temple guards went back to the chief priests and the Pharisees, who
asked them, "Why didn't you bring him in?"

46"No one ever spoke the way this man does," the guards replied.

47"You mean he has deceived you also?" the Pharisees retorted. 48"Have any of
the rulers or of the Pharisees believed in him? 49No! But this mob that knows noth-
ing of the law — there is a curse on them."

50Nicodemus, who had gone to Jesus earlier and who was one of their own num-
ber, asked, 51"Does our law condemn a man without first hearing him to find out
what he has been doing?"

52They replied, "Are you from Galilee, too? Look into it, and you will find that a
prophet does not come out of Galilee."

[a] *37,38 Or me. And let anyone drink 38who believes in me." As Scripture has said, "Out of him* (or *them*) *will flow rivers of living water."*

[The earliest manuscripts and many other ancient witnesses do not have John 7:53—8:11. A few
manuscripts include these verses, wholly or in part, after John 7:36, John 21:25, Luke 21:38 or Luke 24:53.]

8 *53 Then they all went home, 1 but Jesus went to the Mount of Olives.*
2 At dawn he appeared again in the temple courts, where all the people gathered around him, and
he sat down to teach them. 3 The teachers of the law and the Pharisees brought in a woman caught in
adultery. They made her stand before the group 4 and said to Jesus, "Teacher, this woman was caught
in the act of adultery. 5 In the Law Moses commanded us to stone such women. Now what do you say?"
6 They were using this question as a trap, in order to have a basis for accusing him.
But Jesus bent down and started to write on the ground with his finger. 7 When they kept on ques-
tioning him, he straightened up and said to them, "Let any one of you who is without sin be the first
to throw a stone at her." 8 Again he stooped down and wrote on the ground.
9 At this, those who heard began to go away one at a time, the older ones first, until only Jesus was
left, with the woman still standing there. 10 Jesus straightened up and asked her, "Woman, where are
they? Has no one condemned you?"
11 "No one, sir," she said.
"Then neither do I condemn you," Jesus declared. "Go now and leave your life of sin."

Dispute Over Jesus' Testimony

12 When Jesus spoke again to the people, he said, "I am the light of the world.
Whoever follows me will never walk in darkness, but will have the light of life."
13 The Pharisees challenged him, "Here you are, appearing as your own witness;
your testimony is not valid."
14 Jesus answered, "Even if I testify on my own behalf, my testimony is valid, for I
know where I came from and where I am going. But you have no idea where I come
from or where I am going. 15 You judge by human standards; I pass judgment on
no one. 16 But if I do judge, my decisions are true, because I am not alone. I stand
with the Father, who sent me. 17 In your own Law it is written that the testimony of
two witnesses is true. 18 I am one who testifies for myself; my other witness is the
Father, who sent me."
19 Then they asked him, "Where is your father?"
"You do not know me or my Father," Jesus replied. "If you knew me, you would
know my Father also." 20 He spoke these words while teaching in the temple courts
near the place where the offerings were put. Yet no one seized him, because his
hour had not yet come.

Dispute Over Who Jesus Is

21 Once more Jesus said to them, "I am going away, and you will look for me, and
you will die in your sin. Where I go, you cannot come."
22 This made the Jews ask, "Will he kill himself? Is that why he says, 'Where I go,
you cannot come'?"
23 But he continued, "You are from below; I am from above. You are of this world;
I am not of this world. 24 I told you that you would die in your sins; if you do not be-
lieve that I am he, you will indeed die in your sins."
25 "Who are you?" they asked.
"Just what I have been telling you from the beginning," Jesus replied. 26 "I have
much to say in judgment of you. But he who sent me is trustworthy, and what I have
heard from him I tell the world."

27They did not understand that he was telling them about his Father. 28So Jesus
said, "When you have lifted up[a] the Son of Man, then you will know that I am he and
that I do nothing on my own but speak just what the Father has taught me. 29The
one who sent me is with me; he has not left me alone, for I always do what pleases
him." 30Even as he spoke, many believed in him.

Dispute Over Whose Children Jesus' Opponents Are

31To the Jews who had believed him, Jesus said, "If you hold to my teaching, you
are really my disciples. 32Then you will know the truth, and the truth will set you free."
33They answered him, "We are Abraham's descendants and have never been
slaves of anyone. How can you say that we shall be set free?"
34Jesus replied, "Very truly I tell you, everyone who sins is a slave to sin. 35Now a
slave has no permanent place in the family, but a son belongs to it forever. 36So if
the Son sets you free, you will be free indeed. 37I know that you are Abraham's de-
scendants. Yet you are looking for a way to kill me, because you have no room for
my word. 38I am telling you what I have seen in the Father's presence, and you are
doing what you have heard from your father.[b]"
39"Abraham is our father," they answered.
"If you were Abraham's children," said Jesus, "then you would[c] do what Abraham
did. 40As it is, you are looking for a way to kill me, a man who has told you the truth
that I heard from God. Abraham did not do such things. 41You are doing the works
of your own father."
"We are not illegitimate children," they protested. "The only Father we have is
God himself."
42Jesus said to them, "If God were your Father, you would love me, for I have
come here from God. I have not come on my own; God sent me. 43Why is my lan-
guage not clear to you? Because you are unable to hear what I say. 44You belong
to your father, the devil, and you want to carry out your father's desires. He was
a murderer from the beginning, not holding to the truth, for there is no truth in
him. When he lies, he speaks his native language, for he is a liar and the father of
lies. 45Yet because I tell the truth, you do not believe me! 46Can any of you prove
me guilty of sin? If I am telling the truth, why don't you believe me? 47Whoever be-
longs to God hears what God says. The reason you do not hear is that you do not
belong to God."

Jesus' Claims About Himself

48The Jews answered him, "Aren't we right in saying that you are a Samaritan
and demon-possessed?"
49"I am not possessed by a demon," said Jesus, "but I honor my Father and you
dishonor me. 50I am not seeking glory for myself; but there is one who seeks it,
and he is the judge. 51Very truly I tell you, whoever obeys my word will never see
death."
52At this they exclaimed, "Now we know that you are demon-possessed! Abra-
ham died and so did the prophets, yet you say that whoever obeys your word will
never taste death. 53Are you greater than our father Abraham? He died, and so did
the prophets. Who do you think you are?"

[a] *28* The Greek for *lifted up* also means *exalted.* [b] *38* Or *presence. Therefore do what you have heard from the Father.* [c] *39* Some early manuscripts *"If you are Abraham's children," said Jesus, "then*

54 Jesus replied, "If I glorify myself, my glory means nothing. My Father, whom
you claim as your God, is the one who glorifies me. 55 Though you do not know him,
I know him. If I said I did not, I would be a liar like you, but I do know him and obey
his word. 56 Your father Abraham rejoiced at the thought of seeing my day; he saw
it and was glad."
57 "You are not yet fifty years old," they said to him, "and you have seen Abraham!"
58 "Very truly I tell you," Jesus answered, "before Abraham was born, I am!" 59 At
this, they picked up stones to stone him, but Jesus hid himself, slipping away from
the temple grounds.

Jesus Heals a Man Born Blind

9 As he went along, he saw a man blind from birth. 2 His disciples asked him,
"Rabbi, who sinned, this man or his parents, that he was born blind?"
3 "Neither this man nor his parents sinned," said Jesus, "but this happened so that
the works of God might be displayed in him. 4 As long as it is day, we must do the
works of him who sent me. Night is coming, when no one can work. 5 While I am in
the world, I am the light of the world."
6 After saying this, he spit on the ground, made some mud with the saliva, and
put it on the man's eyes. 7 "Go," he told him, "wash in the Pool of Siloam" (this word
means "Sent"). So the man went and washed, and came home seeing.
8 His neighbors and those who had formerly seen him begging asked, "Isn't this
the same man who used to sit and beg?" 9 Some claimed that he was.
Others said, "No, he only looks like him."
But he himself insisted, "I am the man."
10 "How then were your eyes opened?" they asked.
11 He replied, "The man they call Jesus made some mud and put it on my eyes.
He told me to go to Siloam and wash. So I went and washed, and then I could see."
12 "Where is this man?" they asked him.
"I don't know," he said.

The Pharisees Investigate the Healing

13 They brought to the Pharisees the man who had been blind. 14 Now the day on
which Jesus had made the mud and opened the man's eyes was a Sabbath. 15 There-
fore the Pharisees also asked him how he had received his sight. "He put mud on
my eyes," the man replied, "and I washed, and now I see."
16 Some of the Pharisees said, "This man is not from God, for he does not keep
the Sabbath."
But others asked, "How can a sinner perform such signs?" So they were divided.
17 Then they turned again to the blind man, "What have you to say about him? It
was your eyes he opened."
The man replied, "He is a prophet."
18 They still did not believe that he had been blind and had received his sight until
they sent for the man's parents. 19 "Is this your son?" they asked. "Is this the one you
say was born blind? How is it that now he can see?"
20 "We know he is our son," the parents answered, "and we know he was born
blind. 21 But how he can see now, or who opened his eyes, we don't know. Ask him. He
is of age; he will speak for himself." 22 His parents said this because they were afraid
of the Jewish leaders, who already had decided that anyone who acknowledged

Is Sickness Punishment?

Read John 9:1–7. Some people think that all sickness is punishment for sin. What did Jesus say about this idea in verse 3? Jesus healed the man and called healing "the works of [God] who sent me" (John 9:4).

Doctors, nurses, and many others work for the healing of sick people. If there is a doctor or nurse in your church, or if your church supports a medical missionary, talk to him or her about this Bible story. Ask that person how being a doctor or nurse is doing God's work and write their response below.

John 9:1–7

that Jesus was the Messiah would be put out of the synagogue. 23That was why his
parents said, “He is of age; ask him.”
24A second time they summoned the man who had been blind. “Give glory to God
by telling the truth,” they said. “We know this man is a sinner.”
25He replied, “Whether he is a sinner or not, I don’t know. One thing I do know. I
was blind but now I see!”
26Then they asked him, “What did he do to you? How did he open your eyes?”
27He answered, “I have told you already and you did not listen. Why do you want
to hear it again? Do you want to become his disciples too?”
28Then they hurled insults at him and said, “You are this fellow’s disciple! We are
disciples of Moses! 29We know that God spoke to Moses, but as for this fellow, we
don’t even know where he comes from.”
30The man answered, “Now that is remarkable! You don’t know where he comes
from, yet he opened my eyes. 31We know that God does not listen to sinners. He
listens to the godly person who does his will. 32Nobody has ever heard of opening
the eyes of a man born blind. 33If this man were not from God, he could do nothing.”
34To this they replied, “You were steeped in sin at birth; how dare you lecture us!”
And they threw him out.

Spiritual Blindness

35Jesus heard that they had thrown him out, and when he found him, he said, “Do
you believe in the Son of Man?”
36“Who is he, sir?” the man asked. “Tell me so that I may believe in him.”
37Jesus said, “You have now seen him; in fact, he is the one speaking with you.”
38Then the man said, “Lord, I believe,” and he worshiped him.
39Jesus said,[a] “For judgment I have come into this world, so that the blind will see
and those who see will become blind.”
40Some Pharisees who were with him heard him say this and asked, “What? Are
we blind too?”
41Jesus said, “If you were blind, you would not be guilty of sin; but now that you
claim you can see, your guilt remains.

The Good Shepherd and His Sheep

10 “Very truly I tell you Pharisees, anyone who does not enter the sheep pen by
the gate, but climbs in by some other way, is a thief and a robber. 2The one
who enters by the gate is the shepherd of the sheep. 3The gatekeeper opens the
gate for him, and the sheep listen to his voice. He calls his own sheep by name and
leads them out. 4When he has brought out all his own, he goes on ahead of them,
and his sheep follow him because they know his voice. 5But they will never follow
a stranger; in fact, they will run away from him because they do not recognize a
stranger’s voice.” 6Jesus used this figure of speech, but the Pharisees did not un-
derstand what he was telling them.
7Therefore Jesus said again, “Very truly I tell you, I am the gate for the sheep. 8All
who have come before me are thieves and robbers, but the sheep have not listened
to them. 9I am the gate; whoever enters through me will be saved.[b] They will come
in and go out, and find pasture. 10The thief comes only to steal and kill and destroy;
I have come that they may have life, and have it to the full.

[a] *38,39* Some early manuscripts do not have *Then the man said . . . 39Jesus said.* [b] *9* Or *kept safe*

Life in Bible Times

The Sheep Pen

At night flocks of sheep were kept in pens made of rocks or branches with thorns. As the sheep went into the pen, the shepherd counted them to see whether any were missing. The shepherd slept in the only doorway. If wild animals came near, the shepherd was there to protect the sheep.

11"I am the good shepherd. The good shepherd lays down his life for the sheep.
12The hired hand is not the shepherd and does not own the sheep. So when he sees
the wolf coming, he abandons the sheep and runs away. Then the wolf attacks the
flock and scatters it. 13The man runs away because he is a hired hand and cares
nothing for the sheep.

14"I am the good shepherd; I know my sheep and my sheep know me — 15just as
the Father knows me and I know the Father — and I lay down my life for the sheep.
16I have other sheep that are not of this sheep pen. I must bring them also. They too
will listen to my voice, and there shall be one flock and one shepherd. 17The reason
my Father loves me is that I lay down my life — only to take it up again. 18No one
takes it from me, but I lay it down of my own accord. I have authority to lay it down
and authority to take it up again. This command I received from my Father."

19The Jews who heard these words were again divided. 20Many of them said, "He
is demon-possessed and raving mad. Why listen to him?"

21But others said, "These are not the sayings of a man possessed by a demon. Can
a demon open the eyes of the blind?"

Further Conflict Over Jesus' Claims

22Then came the Festival of Dedication[a] at Jerusalem. It was winter, 23and Jesus
was in the temple courts walking in Solomon's Colonnade. 24The Jews who were
there gathered around him, saying, "How long will you keep us in suspense? If you
are the Messiah, tell us plainly."

25Jesus answered, "I did tell you, but you do not believe. The works I do in my
Father's name testify about me, 26but you do not believe because you are not my
sheep. 27My sheep listen to my voice; I know them, and they follow me. 28I give them
eternal life, and they shall never perish; no one will snatch them out of my hand.
29My Father, who has given them to me, is greater than all[b]; no one can snatch them
out of my Father's hand. 30I and the Father are one."

31Again his Jewish opponents picked up stones to stone him, 32but Jesus said to
them, "I have shown you many good works from the Father. For which of these do
you stone me?"

33"We are not stoning you for any good work," they replied, "but for blasphemy,
because you, a mere man, claim to be God."

34Jesus answered them, "Is it not written in your Law, 'I have said you are
"gods"'[c]? 35If he called them 'gods,' to whom the word of God came — and Scripture
cannot be set aside — 36what about the one whom the Father set apart as his very
own and sent into the world? Why then do you accuse me of blasphemy because I
said, 'I am God's Son'? 37Do not believe me unless I do the works of my Father. 38But
if I do them, even though you do not believe me, believe the works, that you may
know and understand that the Father is in me, and I in the Father." 39Again they
tried to seize him, but he escaped their grasp.

40Then Jesus went back across the Jordan to the place where John had been
baptizing in the early days. There he stayed, 41and many people came to him. They
said, "Though John never performed a sign, all that John said about this man was
true." 42And in that place many believed in Jesus.

[a] *22* That is, Hanukkah [b] *29* Many early manuscripts *What my Father has given me is greater than all*
[c] *34* Psalm 82:6

The Death of Lazarus

11 Now a man named Lazarus was sick. He was from Bethany, the village of Mary
and her sister Martha. 2(This Mary, whose brother Lazarus now lay sick, was the
same one who poured perfume on the Lord and wiped his feet with her hair.) 3So
the sisters sent word to Jesus, "Lord, the one you love is sick."
4When he heard this, Jesus said, "This sickness will not end in death. No, it is
for God's glory so that God's Son may be glorified through it." 5Now Jesus loved
Martha and her sister and Lazarus. 6So when he heard that Lazarus was sick, he
stayed where he was two more days, 7and then he said to his disciples, "Let us go
back to Judea."
8"But Rabbi," they said, "a short while ago the Jews there tried to stone you, and
yet you are going back?"
9Jesus answered, "Are there not twelve hours of daylight? Anyone who walks in
the daytime will not stumble, for they see by this world's light. 10It is when a person
walks at night that they stumble, for they have no light."
11After he had said this, he went on to tell them, "Our friend Lazarus has fallen
asleep; but I am going there to wake him up."
12His disciples replied, "Lord, if he sleeps, he will get better." 13Jesus had been
speaking of his death, but his disciples thought he meant natural sleep.
14So then he told them plainly, "Lazarus is dead, 15and for your sake I am glad I
was not there, so that you may believe. But let us go to him."
16Then Thomas (also known as Didymus[a]) said to the rest of the disciples, "Let us
also go, that we may die with him."

Jesus Comforts the Sisters of Lazarus

17On his arrival, Jesus found that Lazarus had already been in the tomb for four
days. 18Now Bethany was less than two miles[b] from Jerusalem, 19and many Jews
had come to Martha and Mary to comfort them in the loss of their brother. 20When
Martha heard that Jesus was coming, she went out to meet him, but Mary stayed
at home.
21"Lord," Martha said to Jesus, "if you had been here, my brother would not have
died. 22But I know that even now God will give you whatever you ask."
23Jesus said to her, "Your brother will rise again."
24Martha answered, "I know he will rise again in the resurrection at the last day."
25Jesus said to her, "I am the resurrection and the life. The one who believes in
me will live, even though they die; 26and whoever lives by believing in me will never
die. Do you believe this?"
27"Yes, Lord," she replied, "I believe that you are the Messiah, the Son of God, who
is to come into the world."
28After she had said this, she went back and called her sister Mary aside. "The
Teacher is here," she said, "and is asking for you." 29When Mary heard this, she got
up quickly and went to him. 30Now Jesus had not yet entered the village, but was
still at the place where Martha had met him. 31When the Jews who had been with
Mary in the house, comforting her, noticed how quickly she got up and went out,
they followed her, supposing she was going to the tomb to mourn there.

[a] *16* *Thomas* (Aramaic) and *Didymus* (Greek) both mean *twin*. [b] *18* Or about 3 kilometers

32When Mary reached the place where Jesus was and saw him, she fell at his feet
and said, "Lord, if you had been here, my brother would not have died."
33When Jesus saw her weeping, and the Jews who had come along with her also
weeping, he was deeply moved in spirit and troubled. 34"Where have you laid him?"
he asked.
"Come and see, Lord," they replied.
35Jesus wept.
36Then the Jews said, "See how he loved him!"
37But some of them said, "Could not he who opened the eyes of the blind man
have kept this man from dying?"

Jesus Raises Lazarus From the Dead

38Jesus, once more deeply moved, came to the tomb. It was a cave with a stone
laid across the entrance. 39"Take away the stone," he said.
"But, Lord," said Martha, the sister of the dead man, "by this time there is a bad
odor, for he has been there four days."
40Then Jesus said, "Did I not tell you that if you believe, you will see the glory of God?"
41So they took away the stone. Then Jesus looked up and said, "Father, I thank
you that you have heard me. 42I knew that you always hear me, but I said this for
the benefit of the people standing here, that they may believe that you sent me."
43When he had said this, Jesus called in a loud voice, "Lazarus, come out!" 44The
dead man came out, his hands and feet wrapped with strips of linen, and a cloth
around his face.
Jesus said to them, "Take off the grave clothes and let him go."

The Plot to Kill Jesus

45Therefore many of the Jews who had come to visit Mary, and had seen what
Jesus did, believed in him. 46But some of them went to the Pharisees and told them
what Jesus had done. 47Then the chief priests and the Pharisees called a meeting
of the Sanhedrin.
"What are we accomplishing?" they asked. "Here is this man performing many
signs. 48If we let him go on like this, everyone will believe in him, and then the Ro-
mans will come and take away both our temple and our nation."
49Then one of them, named Caiaphas, who was high priest that year, spoke up,
"You know nothing at all! 50You do not realize that it is better for you that one man
die for the people than that the whole nation perish."
51He did not say this on his own, but as high priest that year he prophesied that
Jesus would die for the Jewish nation, 52and not only for that nation but also for the
scattered children of God, to bring them together and make them one. 53So from
that day on they plotted to take his life.
54Therefore Jesus no longer moved about publicly among the people of Judea.
Instead he withdrew to a region near the wilderness, to a village called Ephraim,
where he stayed with his disciples.
55When it was almost time for the Jewish Passover, many went up from the coun-
try to Jerusalem for their ceremonial cleansing before the Passover. 56They kept
looking for Jesus, and as they stood in the temple courts they asked one another,
"What do you think? Isn't he coming to the festival at all?" 57But the chief priests
and the Pharisees had given orders that anyone who found out where Jesus was
should report it so that they might arrest him.

Jesus Anointed at Bethany

12 Six days before the Passover, Jesus came to Bethany, where Lazarus lived, whom
Jesus had raised from the dead. 2Here a dinner was given in Jesus' honor. Martha
served, while Lazarus was among those reclining at the table with him. 3Then Mary
took about a pint[a] of pure nard, an expensive perfume; she poured it on Jesus' feet and
wiped his feet with her hair. And the house was filled with the fragrance of the perfume.
4But one of his disciples, Judas Iscariot, who was later to betray him, objected,
5"Why wasn't this perfume sold and the money given to the poor? It was worth a year's
wages.[b]" 6He did not say this because he cared about the poor but because he was
a thief; as keeper of the money bag, he used to help himself to what was put into it.
7"Leave her alone," Jesus replied. "It was intended that she should save this per-
fume for the day of my burial. 8You will always have the poor among you,[c] but you
will not always have me."
9Meanwhile a large crowd of Jews found out that Jesus was there and came, not
only because of him but also to see Lazarus, whom he had raised from the dead.
10So the chief priests made plans to kill Lazarus as well, 11for on account of him
many of the Jews were going over to Jesus and believing in him.

Jesus Comes to Jerusalem as King

12The next day the great crowd that had come for the festival heard that Jesus
was on his way to Jerusalem. 13They took palm branches and went out to meet
him, shouting,

"Hosanna![d]"

"Blessed is he who comes in the name of the Lord!"[e]

"Blessed is the king of Israel!"

14Jesus found a young donkey and sat on it, as it is written:

15"Do not be afraid, Daughter Zion;
see, your king is coming,
seated on a donkey's colt."[f]

16At first his disciples did not understand all this. Only after Jesus was glorified
did they realize that these things had been written about him and that these things
had been done to him.
17Now the crowd that was with him when he called Lazarus from the tomb and
raised him from the dead continued to spread the word. 18Many people, because
they had heard that he had performed this sign, went out to meet him. 19So the
Pharisees said to one another, "See, this is getting us nowhere. Look how the whole
world has gone after him!"

Jesus Predicts His Death

20Now there were some Greeks among those who went up to worship at the
festival. 21They came to Philip, who was from Bethsaida in Galilee, with a request.
"Sir," they said, "we would like to see Jesus." 22Philip went to tell Andrew; Andrew
and Philip in turn told Jesus.

[a] *3* Or about 0.5 liter [b] *5* Greek *three hundred denarii* [c] *8* See Deut. 15:11. [d] *13* A Hebrew expression meaning "Save!" which became an exclamation of praise [e] *13* Psalm 118:25,26 [f] *15* Zech. 9:9

23 Jesus replied, "The hour has come for the Son of Man to be glorified. 24 Very truly
I tell you, unless a kernel of wheat falls to the ground and dies, it remains only a
single seed. But if it dies, it produces many seeds. 25 Anyone who loves their life will
lose it, while anyone who hates their life in this world will keep it for eternal life.
26 Whoever serves me must follow me; and where I am, my servant also will be. My
Father will honor the one who serves me.

27 "Now my soul is troubled, and what shall I say? 'Father, save me from this hour'?
No, it was for this very reason I came to this hour. 28 Father, glorify your name!"

Then a voice came from heaven, "I have glorified it, and will glorify it again."
29 The crowd that was there and heard it said it had thundered; others said an an-
gel had spoken to him.

30 Jesus said, "This voice was for your benefit, not mine. 31 Now is the time for judg-
ment on this world; now the prince of this world will be driven out. 32 And I, when I
am lifted up[a] from the earth, will draw all people to myself." 33 He said this to show
the kind of death he was going to die.

34 The crowd spoke up, "We have heard from the Law that the Messiah will re-
main forever, so how can you say, 'The Son of Man must be lifted up'? Who is this
'Son of Man'?"

35 Then Jesus told them, "You are going to have the light just a little while longer.
Walk while you have the light, before darkness overtakes you. Whoever walks in the
dark does not know where they are going. 36 Believe in the light while you have the
light, so that you may become children of light." When he had finished speaking,
Jesus left and hid himself from them.

Belief and Unbelief Among the Jews

37 Even after Jesus had performed so many signs in their presence, they still would
not believe in him. 38 This was to fulfill the word of Isaiah the prophet:

> "Lord, who has believed our message
> and to whom has the arm of the Lord been revealed?"[b]

39 For this reason they could not believe, because, as Isaiah says elsewhere:

> 40 "He has blinded their eyes
> and hardened their hearts,
> so they can neither see with their eyes,
> nor understand with their hearts,
> nor turn — and I would heal them."[c]

41 Isaiah said this because he saw Jesus' glory and spoke about him.

42 Yet at the same time many even among the leaders believed in him. But be-
cause of the Pharisees they would not openly acknowledge their faith for fear they
would be put out of the synagogue; 43 for they loved human praise more than praise
from God.

44 Then Jesus cried out, "Whoever believes in me does not believe in me only, but
in the one who sent me. 45 The one who looks at me is seeing the one who sent me.
46 I have come into the world as a light, so that no one who believes in me should
stay in darkness.

[a] *32* The Greek for *lifted up* also means *exalted.* [b] *38* Isaiah 53:1 [c] *40* Isaiah 6:10

47“If anyone hears my words but does not keep them, I do not judge that person.
For I did not come to judge the world, but to save the world. 48There is a judge for
the one who rejects me and does not accept my words; the very words I have spo-
ken will condemn them at the last day. 49For I did not speak on my own, but the
Father who sent me commanded me to say all that I have spoken. 50I know that his
command leads to eternal life. So whatever I say is just what the Father has told
me to say.”

Jesus Washes His Disciples’ Feet

13 It was just before the Passover Festival. Jesus knew that the hour had come
for him to leave this world and go to the Father. Having loved his own who
were in the world, he loved them to the end.
2The evening meal was in progress, and the devil had already prompted Judas,
the son of Simon Iscariot, to betray Jesus. 3Jesus knew that the Father had put
all things under his power, and that he had come from God and was returning to
God; 4so he got up from the meal, took off his outer clothing, and wrapped a towel
around his waist. 5After that, he poured water into a basin and began to wash his
disciples’ feet, drying them with the towel that was wrapped around him.
6He came to Simon Peter, who said to him, “Lord, are you going to wash my feet?”
7Jesus replied, “You do not realize now what I am doing, but later you will un-
derstand.”
8“No,” said Peter, “you shall never wash my feet.”
Jesus answered, “Unless I wash you, you have no part with me.”
9“Then, Lord,” Simon Peter replied, “not just my feet but my hands and my head
as well!”
10Jesus answered, “Those who have had a bath need only to wash their feet;
their whole body is clean. And you are clean, though not every one of you.” 11For
he knew who was going to betray him, and that was why he said not every one
was clean.
12When he had finished washing their feet, he put on his clothes and returned to
his place. “Do you understand what I have done for you?” he asked them. 13“You
call me ‘Teacher’ and ‘Lord,’ and rightly so, for that is what I am. 14Now that I, your
Lord and Teacher, have washed your feet, you also should wash one another’s
feet. 15I have set you an example that you should do as I have done for you. 16Very
truly I tell you, no servant is greater than his master, nor is a messenger greater
than the one who sent him. 17Now that you know these things, you will be blessed
if you do them.

Jesus Predicts His Betrayal

18“I am not referring to all of you; I know those I have chosen. But this is to fulfill
this passage of Scripture: ‘He who shared my bread has turned[a] against me.’[b]
19“I am telling you now before it happens, so that when it does happen you will
believe that I am who I am. 20Very truly I tell you, whoever accepts anyone I send
accepts me; and whoever accepts me accepts the one who sent me.”
21After he had said this, Jesus was troubled in spirit and testified, “Very truly I tell
you, one of you is going to betray me.”

[a] *18* Greek *has lifted up his heel* [b] *18* Psalm 41:9

Life in Bible Times

Foot Washing

When visitors came into a house, they took off their sandals. A good host made water available to wash their dusty feet. Usually the lowest servant in the house was ordered to wash the guests' feet. Jesus was showing us how to be humble when he took the job of washing his disciples' feet.

22His disciples stared at one another, at a loss to know which of them he meant.
23One of them, the disciple whom Jesus loved, was reclining next to him. 24Simon
Peter motioned to this disciple and said, “Ask him which one he means.”
25Leaning back against Jesus, he asked him, “Lord, who is it?”
26Jesus answered, “It is the one to whom I will give this piece of bread when I
have dipped it in the dish.” Then, dipping the piece of bread, he gave it to Judas, the
son of Simon Iscariot. 27As soon as Judas took the bread, Satan entered into him.
So Jesus told him, “What you are about to do, do quickly.” 28But no one at the
meal understood why Jesus said this to him. 29Since Judas had charge of the mon-
ey, some thought Jesus was telling him to buy what was needed for the festival,
or to give something to the poor. 30As soon as Judas had taken the bread, he went
out. And it was night.

Jesus Predicts Peter's Denial

31When he was gone, Jesus said, “Now the Son of Man is glorified and God is
glorified in him. 32If God is glorified in him,[a] God will glorify the Son in himself, and
will glorify him at once.
33“My children, I will be with you only a little longer. You will look for me, and just
as I told the Jews, so I tell you now: Where I am going, you cannot come.
34“A new command I give you: Love one another. As I have loved you, so you must
love one another. 35By this everyone will know that you are my disciples, if you love
one another.”
36Simon Peter asked him, “Lord, where are you going?”
Jesus replied, “Where I am going, you cannot follow now, but you will follow later.”
37Peter asked, “Lord, why can't I follow you now? I will lay down my life for you.”
38Then Jesus answered, “Will you really lay down your life for me? Very truly I tell
you, before the rooster crows, you will disown me three times!

Jesus Comforts His Disciples

14 “Do not let your hearts be troubled. You believe in God[b]; believe also in me.
2My Father's house has many rooms; if that were not so, would I have told you
that I am going there to prepare a place for you? 3And if I go and prepare a place
for you, I will come back and take you to be with me that you also may be where I
am. 4You know the way to the place where I am going.”

Jesus the Way to the Father

5Thomas said to him, “Lord, we don't know where you are going, so how can we
know the way?”
6Jesus answered, “I am the way and the truth and the life. No one comes to the
Father except through me. 7If you really know me, you will know[c] my Father as well.
From now on, you do know him and have seen him.”
8Philip said, “Lord, show us the Father and that will be enough for us.”
9Jesus answered: “Don't you know me, Philip, even after I have been among you
such a long time? Anyone who has seen me has seen the Father. How can you say,
'Show us the Father'? 10Don't you believe that I am in the Father, and that the Father
is in me? The words I say to you I do not speak on my own authority. Rather, it is
the Father, living in me, who is doing his work. 11Believe me when I say that I am in

[a] *32* Many early manuscripts do not have *If God is glorified in him.* [b] *1* Or *Believe in God* [c] *7* Some manuscripts *If you really knew me, you would know*

One Way

Read John 14:1–7. There are many religions in the world. Most teach that people must live good lives in order to go to heaven. What is special about Christianity is the truth that eternal life is a gift, a gift only Jesus can give a person.

In the journal space below, write the word "ONE" in bubble letters. Inside the bubble letters, draw pictures or write Bible verses that show Jesus as the one and only way to eternal life. (Ideas: John 3:16, picture of a cross, picture of a stone rolled away, etc.)

Live It!

John 14:1–7

the Father and the Father is in me; or at least believe on the evidence of the works
themselves. 12Very truly I tell you, whoever believes in me will do the works I have
been doing, and they will do even greater things than these, because I am going
to the Father. 13And I will do whatever you ask in my name, so that the Father may
be glorified in the Son. 14You may ask me for anything in my name, and I will do it.

Jesus Promises the Holy Spirit

15"If you love me, keep my commands. 16And I will ask the Father, and he will give
you another advocate to help you and be with you forever— 17the Spirit of truth.
The world cannot accept him, because it neither sees him nor knows him. But you
know him, for he lives with you and will be[a] in you. 18I will not leave you as orphans;
I will come to you. 19Before long, the world will not see me anymore, but you will
see me. Because I live, you also will live. 20On that day you will realize that I am in
my Father, and you are in me, and I am in you. 21Whoever has my commands and
keeps them is the one who loves me. The one who loves me will be loved by my Fa-
ther, and I too will love them and show myself to them."

22Then Judas (not Judas Iscariot) said, "But, Lord, why do you intend to show
yourself to us and not to the world?"

23Jesus replied, "Anyone who loves me will obey my teaching. My Father will love
them, and we will come to them and make our home with them. 24Anyone who
does not love me will not obey my teaching. These words you hear are not my own;
they belong to the Father who sent me.

25"All this I have spoken while still with you. 26But the Advocate, the Holy Spirit,
whom the Father will send in my name, will teach you all things and will remind
you of everything I have said to you. 27Peace I leave with you; my peace I give you.
I do not give to you as the world gives. Do not let your hearts be troubled and do
not be afraid.

28"You heard me say, 'I am going away and I am coming back to you.' If you loved
me, you would be glad that I am going to the Father, for the Father is greater than
I. 29I have told you now before it happens, so that when it does happen you will
believe. 30I will not say much more to you, for the prince of this world is coming.
He has no hold over me, 31but he comes so that the world may learn that I love the
Father and do exactly what my Father has commanded me.

"Come now; let us leave.

The Vine and the Branches

15 "I am the true vine, and my Father is the gardener. 2He cuts off every branch in
me that bears no fruit, while every branch that does bear fruit he prunes[b] so
that it will be even more fruitful. 3You are already clean because of the word I have
spoken to you. 4Remain in me, as I also remain in you. No branch can bear fruit by
itself; it must remain in the vine. Neither can you bear fruit unless you remain in me.

5"I am the vine; you are the branches. If you remain in me and I in you, you will
bear much fruit; apart from me you can do nothing. 6If you do not remain in me,
you are like a branch that is thrown away and withers; such branches are picked
up, thrown into the fire and burned. 7If you remain in me and my words remain in
you, ask whatever you wish, and it will be done for you. 8This is to my Father's glory,
that you bear much fruit, showing yourselves to be my disciples.

[a] *17* Some early manuscripts *and is* [b] *2* The Greek for *he prunes* also means *he cleans.*

Help When We Need It Most

Live It!

Who is the Christian's helper? Read John 14:15–21 to find out.

God the Holy Spirit is our invisible helper. He is in us and stays with us. When we need strength to obey God's commands, the Holy Spirit strengthens us.

Paste a photograph of yourself in the journal space below. Then draw a big, bright circle around your photograph. Let the picture remind you that God is with you, to give you strength to do right.

John 14:15–21

[9]“As the Father has loved me, so have I loved you. Now remain in my love. [10]If
you keep my commands, you will remain in my love, just as I have kept my Father’s
commands and remain in his love. [11]I have told you this so that my joy may be in
you and that your joy may be complete. [12]My command is this: Love each other
as I have loved you. [13]Greater love has no one than this: to lay down one’s life for
one’s friends. [14]You are my friends if you do what I command. [15]I no longer call you
servants, because a servant does not know his master’s business. Instead, I have
called you friends, for everything that I learned from my Father I have made known
to you. [16]You did not choose me, but I chose you and appointed you so that you
might go and bear fruit — fruit that will last — and so that whatever you ask in my
name the Father will give you. [17]This is my command: Love each other.

The World Hates the Disciples

[18]“If the world hates you, keep in mind that it hated me first. [19]If you belonged to
the world, it would love you as its own. As it is, you do not belong to the world, but
I have chosen you out of the world. That is why the world hates you. [20]Remember
what I told you: ‘A servant is not greater than his master.’[a] If they persecuted me,
they will persecute you also. If they obeyed my teaching, they will obey yours also.
[21]They will treat you this way because of my name, for they do not know the one who
sent me. [22]If I had not come and spoken to them, they would not be guilty of sin; but
now they have no excuse for their sin. [23]Whoever hates me hates my Father as well.
[24]If I had not done among them the works no one else did, they would not be guilty
of sin. As it is, they have seen, and yet they have hated both me and my Father. [25]But
this is to fulfill what is written in their Law: ‘They hated me without reason.’[b]

The Work of the Holy Spirit

[26]“When the Advocate comes, whom I will send to you from the Father — the
Spirit of truth who goes out from the Father — he will testify about me. [27]And you
also must testify, for you have been with me from the beginning.

16 “All this I have told you so that you will not fall away. [2]They will put you out
of the synagogue; in fact, the time is coming when anyone who kills you will
think they are offering a service to God. [3]They will do such things because they have
not known the Father or me. [4]I have told you this, so that when their time comes
you will remember that I warned you about them. I did not tell you this from the be-
ginning because I was with you, [5]but now I am going to him who sent me. None of
you asks me, ‘Where are you going?’ [6]Rather, you are filled with grief because I have
said these things. [7]But very truly I tell you, it is for your good that I am going away.
Unless I go away, the Advocate will not come to you; but if I go, I will send him to
you. [8]When he comes, he will prove the world to be in the wrong about sin and righ-
teousness and judgment: [9]about sin, because people do not believe in me; [10]about
righteousness, because I am going to the Father, where you can see me no longer;
[11]and about judgment, because the prince of this world now stands condemned.

[12]“I have much more to say to you, more than you can now bear. [13]But when he,
the Spirit of truth, comes, he will guide you into all the truth. He will not speak on
his own; he will speak only what he hears, and he will tell you what is yet to come.
[14]He will glorify me because it is from me that he will receive what he will make
known to you. [15]All that belongs to the Father is mine. That is why I said the Spirit
will receive from me what he will make known to you.”

[a] *20* John 13:16 [b] *25* Psalms 35:19; 69:4

The Disciples' Grief Will Turn to Joy

16 Jesus went on to say, "In a little while you will see me no more, and then after
a little while you will see me."
17 At this, some of his disciples said to one another, "What does he mean by say-
ing, 'In a little while you will see me no more, and then after a little while you will
see me,' and 'Because I am going to the Father'?" 18 They kept asking, "What does
he mean by 'a little while'? We don't understand what he is saying."
19 Jesus saw that they wanted to ask him about this, so he said to them, "Are you
asking one another what I meant when I said, 'In a little while you will see me no
more, and then after a little while you will see me'? 20 Very truly I tell you, you will
weep and mourn while the world rejoices. You will grieve, but your grief will turn to
joy. 21 A woman giving birth to a child has pain because her time has come; but when
her baby is born she forgets the anguish because of her joy that a child is born into
the world. 22 So with you: Now is your time of grief, but I will see you again and you
will rejoice, and no one will take away your joy. 23 In that day you will no longer ask
me anything. Very truly I tell you, my Father will give you whatever you ask in my
name. 24 Until now you have not asked for anything in my name. Ask and you will
receive, and your joy will be complete.
25 "Though I have been speaking figuratively, a time is coming when I will no lon-
ger use this kind of language but will tell you plainly about my Father. 26 In that day
you will ask in my name. I am not saying that I will ask the Father on your behalf.
27 No, the Father himself loves you because you have loved me and have believed
that I came from God. 28 I came from the Father and entered the world; now I am
leaving the world and going back to the Father."
29 Then Jesus' disciples said, "Now you are speaking clearly and without figures of
speech. 30 Now we can see that you know all things and that you do not even need
to have anyone ask you questions. This makes us believe that you came from God."
31 "Do you now believe?" Jesus replied. 32 "A time is coming and in fact has come
when you will be scattered, each to your own home. You will leave me all alone. Yet
I am not alone, for my Father is with me.
33 "I have told you these things, so that in me you may have peace. In this world
you will have trouble. But take heart! I have overcome the world."

Jesus Prays to Be Glorified

17 After Jesus said this, he looked toward heaven and prayed:

"Father, the hour has come. Glorify your Son, that your Son may glorify you.
2 For you granted him authority over all people that he might give eternal life to
all those you have given him. 3 Now this is eternal life: that they know you, the
only true God, and Jesus Christ, whom you have sent. 4 I have brought you glory
on earth by finishing the work you gave me to do. 5 And now, Father, glorify me
in your presence with the glory I had with you before the world began.

Jesus Prays for His Disciples

6 "I have revealed you[a] to those whom you gave me out of the world. They
were yours; you gave them to me and they have obeyed your word. 7 Now they
know that everything you have given me comes from you. 8 For I gave them the

[a] 6 Greek *your name*

words you gave me and they accepted them. They knew with certainty that I
came from you, and they believed that you sent me. 9I pray for them. I am not
praying for the world, but for those you have given me, for they are yours. 10All
I have is yours, and all you have is mine. And glory has come to me through
them. 11I will remain in the world no longer, but they are still in the world, and
I am coming to you. Holy Father, protect them by the power of[a] your name,
the name you gave me, so that they may be one as we are one. 12While I was
with them, I protected them and kept them safe by[b] that name you gave me.
None has been lost except the one doomed to destruction so that Scripture
would be fulfilled.

13"I am coming to you now, but I say these things while I am still in the world,
so that they may have the full measure of my joy within them. 14I have given
them your word and the world has hated them, for they are not of the world
any more than I am of the world. 15My prayer is not that you take them out of
the world but that you protect them from the evil one. 16They are not of the
world, even as I am not of it. 17Sanctify them by[c] the truth; your word is truth.
18As you sent me into the world, I have sent them into the world. 19For them I
sanctify myself, that they too may be truly sanctified.

Jesus Prays for All Believers

20"My prayer is not for them alone. I pray also for those who will believe in
me through their message, 21that all of them may be one, Father, just as you
are in me and I am in you. May they also be in us so that the world may believe
that you have sent me. 22I have given them the glory that you gave me, that
they may be one as we are one — 23I in them and you in me — so that they may
be brought to complete unity. Then the world will know that you sent me and
have loved them even as you have loved me.

24"Father, I want those you have given me to be with me where I am, and to
see my glory, the glory you have given me because you loved me before the
creation of the world.

25"Righteous Father, though the world does not know you, I know you, and
they know that you have sent me. 26I have made you[d] known to them, and will
continue to make you known in order that the love you have for me may be in
them and that I myself may be in them."

Jesus Arrested

18 When he had finished praying, Jesus left with his disciples and crossed the
Kidron Valley. On the other side there was a garden, and he and his disciples
went into it.

2Now Judas, who betrayed him, knew the place, because Jesus had often met
there with his disciples. 3So Judas came to the garden, guiding a detachment of
soldiers and some officials from the chief priests and the Pharisees. They were carrying torches, lanterns and weapons.

4Jesus, knowing all that was going to happen to him, went out and asked them,
"Who is it you want?"

5"Jesus of Nazareth," they replied.

[a] *11 Or Father, keep them faithful to* [b] *12 Or kept them faithful to* [c] *17 Or them to live in accordance with* [d] *26 Greek your name*

"I am he," Jesus said. (And Judas the traitor was standing there with them.)
6When Jesus said, "I am he," they drew back and fell to the ground.
7Again he asked them, "Who is it you want?"
"Jesus of Nazareth," they said.
8Jesus answered, "I told you that I am he. If you are looking for me, then let these
men go." 9This happened so that the words he had spoken would be fulfilled: "I
have not lost one of those you gave me."[a]
10Then Simon Peter, who had a sword, drew it and struck the high priest's servant,
cutting off his right ear. (The servant's name was Malchus.)
11Jesus commanded Peter, "Put your sword away! Shall I not drink the cup the
Father has given me?"
12Then the detachment of soldiers with its commander and the Jewish officials
arrested Jesus. They bound him 13and brought him first to Annas, who was the
father-in-law of Caiaphas, the high priest that year. 14Caiaphas was the one who had
advised the Jewish leaders that it would be good if one man died for the people.

Peter's First Denial

15Simon Peter and another disciple were following Jesus. Because this disciple
was known to the high priest, he went with Jesus into the high priest's courtyard,
16but Peter had to wait outside at the door. The other disciple, who was known to
the high priest, came back, spoke to the servant girl on duty there and brought
Peter in.
17"You aren't one of this man's disciples too, are you?" she asked Peter.
He replied, "I am not."
18It was cold, and the servants and officials stood around a fire they had made to
keep warm. Peter also was standing with them, warming himself.

The High Priest Questions Jesus

19Meanwhile, the high priest questioned Jesus about his disciples and his teach-
ing.
20"I have spoken openly to the world," Jesus replied. "I always taught in syna-
gogues or at the temple, where all the Jews come together. I said nothing in secret.
21Why question me? Ask those who heard me. Surely they know what I said."
22When Jesus said this, one of the officials nearby slapped him in the face. "Is this
the way you answer the high priest?" he demanded.
23"If I said something wrong," Jesus replied, "testify as to what is wrong. But if I
spoke the truth, why did you strike me?" 24Then Annas sent him bound to Caiaphas
the high priest.

Peter's Second and Third Denials

25Meanwhile, Simon Peter was still standing there warming himself. So they
asked him, "You aren't one of his disciples too, are you?"
He denied it, saying, "I am not."
26One of the high priest's servants, a relative of the man whose ear Peter had cut
off, challenged him, "Didn't I see you with him in the garden?" 27Again Peter denied
it, and at that moment a rooster began to crow.

[a] 9 John 6:39

Jesus Before Pilate

28Then the Jewish leaders took Jesus from Caiaphas to the palace of the Roman
governor. By now it was early morning, and to avoid ceremonial uncleanness they did
not enter the palace, because they wanted to be able to eat the Passover. 29So Pilate
came out to them and asked, "What charges are you bringing against this man?"
30"If he were not a criminal," they replied, "we would not have handed him over
to you."
31Pilate said, "Take him yourselves and judge him by your own law."
"But we have no right to execute anyone," they objected. 32This took place to
fulfill what Jesus had said about the kind of death he was going to die.
33Pilate then went back inside the palace, summoned Jesus and asked him, "Are
you the king of the Jews?"
34"Is that your own idea," Jesus asked, "or did others talk to you about me?"
35"Am I a Jew?" Pilate replied. "Your own people and chief priests handed you
over to me. What is it you have done?"
36Jesus said, "My kingdom is not of this world. If it were, my servants would fight to
prevent my arrest by the Jewish leaders. But now my kingdom is from another place."
37"You are a king, then!" said Pilate.
Jesus answered, "You say that I am a king. In fact, the reason I was born and
came into the world is to testify to the truth. Everyone on the side of truth listens
to me."
38"What is truth?" retorted Pilate. With this he went out again to the Jews gath-
ered there and said, "I find no basis for a charge against him. 39But it is your custom
for me to release to you one prisoner at the time of the Passover. Do you want me
to release 'the king of the Jews'?"
40They shouted back, "No, not him! Give us Barabbas!" Now Barabbas had taken
part in an uprising.

Jesus Sentenced to Be Crucified

19 Then Pilate took Jesus and had him flogged. 2The soldiers twisted together
a crown of thorns and put it on his head. They clothed him in a purple robe
3and went up to him again and again, saying, "Hail, king of the Jews!" And they
slapped him in the face.
4Once more Pilate came out and said to the Jews gathered there, "Look, I am
bringing him out to you to let you know that I find no basis for a charge against
him." 5When Jesus came out wearing the crown of thorns and the purple robe, Pi-
late said to them, "Here is the man!"
6As soon as the chief priests and their officials saw him, they shouted, "Crucify!
Crucify!"
But Pilate answered, "You take him and crucify him. As for me, I find no basis for
a charge against him."
7The Jewish leaders insisted, "We have a law, and according to that law he must
die, because he claimed to be the Son of God."
8When Pilate heard this, he was even more afraid, 9and he went back inside the
palace. "Where do you come from?" he asked Jesus, but Jesus gave him no answer.
10"Do you refuse to speak to me?" Pilate said. "Don't you realize I have power either
to free you or to crucify you?"

[11]Jesus answered, "You would have no power over me if it were not given to you
from above. Therefore the one who handed me over to you is guilty of a greater sin."
[12]From then on, Pilate tried to set Jesus free, but the Jewish leaders kept shout-
ing, "If you let this man go, you are no friend of Caesar. Anyone who claims to be a
king opposes Caesar."
[13]When Pilate heard this, he brought Jesus out and sat down on the judge's seat
at a place known as the Stone Pavement (which in Aramaic is Gabbatha). [14]It was
the day of Preparation of the Passover; it was about noon.
"Here is your king," Pilate said to the Jews.
[15]But they shouted, "Take him away! Take him away! Crucify him!"
"Shall I crucify your king?" Pilate asked.
"We have no king but Caesar," the chief priests answered.
[16]Finally Pilate handed him over to them to be crucified.

The Crucifixion of Jesus

So the soldiers took charge of Jesus. [17]Carrying his own cross, he went out to the
place of the Skull (which in Aramaic is called Golgotha). [18]There they crucified him,
and with him two others — one on each side and Jesus in the middle.
[19]Pilate had a notice prepared and fastened to the cross. It read: JESUS OF NAZA-
RETH, THE KING OF THE JEWS. [20]Many of the Jews read this sign, for the place where
Jesus was crucified was near the city, and the sign was written in Aramaic, Latin and
Greek. [21]The chief priests of the Jews protested to Pilate, "Do not write 'The King of
the Jews,' but that this man claimed to be king of the Jews."
[22]Pilate answered, "What I have written, I have written."
[23]When the soldiers crucified Jesus, they took his clothes, dividing them into four
shares, one for each of them, with the undergarment remaining. This garment was
seamless, woven in one piece from top to bottom.
[24]"Let's not tear it," they said to one another. "Let's decide by lot who will get it."
This happened that the scripture might be fulfilled that said,

"They divided my clothes among them
and cast lots for my garment."[a]

So this is what the soldiers did.
[25]Near the cross of Jesus stood his mother, his mother's sister, Mary the wife of Clo-
pas, and Mary Magdalene. [26]When Jesus saw his mother there, and the disciple whom
he loved standing nearby, he said to her, "Woman,[b] here is your son," [27]and to the
disciple, "Here is your mother." From that time on, this disciple took her into his home.

The Death of Jesus

[28]Later, knowing that everything had now been finished, and so that Scripture
would be fulfilled, Jesus said, "I am thirsty." [29]A jar of wine vinegar was there, so
they soaked a sponge in it, put the sponge on a stalk of the hyssop plant, and lifted
it to Jesus' lips. [30]When he had received the drink, Jesus said, "It is finished." With
that, he bowed his head and gave up his spirit.
[31]Now it was the day of Preparation, and the next day was to be a special Sab-
bath. Because the Jewish leaders did not want the bodies left on the crosses during
the Sabbath, they asked Pilate to have the legs broken and the bodies taken down.
[32]The soldiers therefore came and broke the legs of the first man who had been

[a] 24 Psalm 22:18 [b] 26 The Greek for *Woman* does not denote any disrespect.

crucified with Jesus, and then those of the other. 33But when they came to Jesus and
found that he was already dead, they did not break his legs. 34Instead, one of the
soldiers pierced Jesus' side with a spear, bringing a sudden flow of blood and water.
35The man who saw it has given testimony, and his testimony is true. He knows that
he tells the truth, and he testifies so that you also may believe. 36These things hap-
pened so that the scripture would be fulfilled: "Not one of his bones will be broken,"[a]
37and, as another scripture says, "They will look on the one they have pierced."[b]

The Burial of Jesus

38Later, Joseph of Arimathea asked Pilate for the body of Jesus. Now Joseph was
a disciple of Jesus, but secretly because he feared the Jewish leaders. With Pilate's
permission, he came and took the body away. 39He was accompanied by Nicode-
mus, the man who earlier had visited Jesus at night. Nicodemus brought a mixture
of myrrh and aloes, about seventy-five pounds.[c] 40Taking Jesus' body, the two of
them wrapped it, with the spices, in strips of linen. This was in accordance with
Jewish burial customs. 41At the place where Jesus was crucified, there was a garden,
and in the garden a new tomb, in which no one had ever been laid. 42Because it was
the Jewish day of Preparation and since the tomb was nearby, they laid Jesus there.

The Empty Tomb

20 Early on the first day of the week, while it was still dark, Mary Magdalene
went to the tomb and saw that the stone had been removed from the en-
trance. 2So she came running to Simon Peter and the other disciple, the one Jesus
loved, and said, "They have taken the Lord out of the tomb, and we don't know
where they have put him!"

3So Peter and the other disciple started for the tomb. 4Both were running, but the
other disciple outran Peter and reached the tomb first. 5He bent over and looked in
at the strips of linen lying there but did not go in. 6Then Simon Peter came along
behind him and went straight into the tomb. He saw the strips of linen lying there,
7as well as the cloth that had been wrapped around Jesus' head. The cloth was
still lying in its place, separate from the linen. 8Finally the other disciple, who had
reached the tomb first, also went inside. He saw and believed. 9(They still did not
understand from Scripture that Jesus had to rise from the dead.) 10Then the disci-
ples went back to where they were staying.

Jesus Appears to Mary Magdalene

11Now Mary stood outside the tomb crying. As she wept, she bent over to look
into the tomb 12and saw two angels in white, seated where Jesus' body had been,
one at the head and the other at the foot.

13They asked her, "Woman, why are you crying?"

"They have taken my Lord away," she said, "and I don't know where they have
put him." 14At this, she turned around and saw Jesus standing there, but she did
not realize that it was Jesus.

15He asked her, "Woman, why are you crying? Who is it you are looking for?"

Thinking he was the gardener, she said, "Sir, if you have carried him away, tell me
where you have put him, and I will get him."

16Jesus said to her, "Mary."

She turned toward him and cried out in Aramaic, "Rabboni!" (which means "Teacher").

[a] *36* Exodus 12:46; Num. 9:12; Psalm 34:20 [b] *37* Zech. 12:10 [c] *39* Or about 34 kilograms

Life in Bible Times

Burial

The Jews buried persons the same day they died. The body was wrapped in strips of cloth and placed in a tomb, often a cave with a large stone in front of the entrance. For some people, sweet-smelling spices were wrapped with the cloth.

17Jesus said, "Do not hold on to me, for I have not yet ascended to the Father. Go
instead to my brothers and tell them, 'I am ascending to my Father and your Father,
to my God and your God.'"
18Mary Magdalene went to the disciples with the news: "I have seen the Lord!"
And she told them that he had said these things to her.

Jesus Appears to His Disciples

19On the evening of that first day of the week, when the disciples were together,
with the doors locked for fear of the Jewish leaders, Jesus came and stood among
them and said, "Peace be with you!" 20After he said this, he showed them his hands
and side. The disciples were overjoyed when they saw the Lord.
21Again Jesus said, "Peace be with you! As the Father has sent me, I am sending
you." 22And with that he breathed on them and said, "Receive the Holy Spirit. 23If
you forgive anyone's sins, their sins are forgiven; if you do not forgive them, they
are not forgiven."

Jesus Appears to Thomas

24Now Thomas (also known as Didymus[a]), one of the Twelve, was not with
the disciples when Jesus came. 25So the other disciples told him, "We have seen
the Lord!"
But he said to them, "Unless I see the nail marks in his hands and put my finger
where the nails were, and put my hand into his side, I will not believe."
26A week later his disciples were in the house again, and Thomas was with them.
Though the doors were locked, Jesus came and stood among them and said,
"Peace be with you!" 27Then he said to Thomas, "Put your finger here; see my hands.
Reach out your hand and put it into my side. Stop doubting and believe."
28Thomas said to him, "My Lord and my God!"
29Then Jesus told him, "Because you have seen me, you have believed; blessed
are those who have not seen and yet have believed."

The Purpose of John's Gospel

30Jesus performed many other signs in the presence of his disciples, which are
not recorded in this book. 31But these are written that you may believe[b] that Jesus
is the Messiah, the Son of God, and that by believing you may have life in his name.

Jesus and the Miraculous Catch of Fish

21 Afterward Jesus appeared again to his disciples, by the Sea of Galilee.[c] It hap-
pened this way: 2Simon Peter, Thomas (also known as Didymus[a]), Nathanael
from Cana in Galilee, the sons of Zebedee, and two other disciples were together.
3"I'm going out to fish," Simon Peter told them, and they said, "We'll go with you."
So they went out and got into the boat, but that night they caught nothing.
4Early in the morning, Jesus stood on the shore, but the disciples did not realize
that it was Jesus.
5He called out to them, "Friends, haven't you any fish?"
"No," they answered.

[a] 24,2 *Thomas* (Aramaic) and *Didymus* (Greek) both mean *twin*. [b] 31 Or *may continue to believe*
[c] 1 Greek *Tiberias*

Life in Bible Times

Fish Symbol

Very early the fish became a symbol of Christianity. During persecution by the Romans, Christians used this symbol as a secret code to discover whether or not another person was a Christian. The letters of the Greek word for fish (*ichthus*) are the same as the first letters in Greek of the words *Jesus Christ*, *God's Son*, and *Savior*.

6 He said, "Throw your net on the right side of the boat and you will find some."
When they did, they were unable to haul the net in because of the large number
of fish.
7 Then the disciple whom Jesus loved said to Peter, "It is the Lord!" As soon as Si-
mon Peter heard him say, "It is the Lord," he wrapped his outer garment around him
(for he had taken it off) and jumped into the water. 8 The other disciples followed
in the boat, towing the net full of fish, for they were not far from shore, about a
hundred yards.[a] 9 When they landed, they saw a fire of burning coals there with fish
on it, and some bread.
10 Jesus said to them, "Bring some of the fish you have just caught." 11 So Simon Pe-
ter climbed back into the boat and dragged the net ashore. It was full of large fish,
153, but even with so many the net was not torn. 12 Jesus said to them, "Come and
have breakfast." None of the disciples dared ask him, "Who are you?" They knew it
was the Lord. 13 Jesus came, took the bread and gave it to them, and did the same
with the fish. 14 This was now the third time Jesus appeared to his disciples after he
was raised from the dead.

Jesus Reinstates Peter

15 When they had finished eating, Jesus said to Simon Peter, "Simon son of John,
do you love me more than these?"

"Yes, Lord," he said, "you know that I love you."

Jesus said, "Feed my lambs."

16 Again Jesus said, "Simon son of John, do you love me?"

He answered, "Yes, Lord, you know that I love you."

Jesus said, "Take care of my sheep."

17 The third time he said to him, "Simon son of John, do you love me?"

Peter was hurt because Jesus asked him the third time, "Do you love me?" He
said, "Lord, you know all things; you know that I love you."

Jesus said, "Feed my sheep. 18 Very truly I tell you, when you were younger you
dressed yourself and went where you wanted; but when you are old you will stretch
out your hands, and someone else will dress you and lead you where you do not
want to go." 19 Jesus said this to indicate the kind of death by which Peter would
glorify God. Then he said to him, "Follow me!"
20 Peter turned and saw that the disciple whom Jesus loved was following them.
(This was the one who had leaned back against Jesus at the supper and had said,
"Lord, who is going to betray you?") 21 When Peter saw him, he asked, "Lord, what
about him?"
22 Jesus answered, "If I want him to remain alive until I return, what is that to you?
You must follow me." 23 Because of this, the rumor spread among the believers that
this disciple would not die. But Jesus did not say that he would not die; he only said,
"If I want him to remain alive until I return, what is that to you?"
24 This is the disciple who testifies to these things and who wrote them down. We
know that his testimony is true.
25 Jesus did many other things as well. If every one of them were written down, I
suppose that even the whole world would not have room for the books that would
be written.

[a] *8* Or about 90 meters

Do You Love Me?

John 21:15-17

The night before Jesus was crucified Peter said three times that he did not even know Jesus. Peter lied because he was afraid. But later Peter was so sorry that he cried (Mark 14:72). After Jesus was raised from the dead, he went to Peter. Read John 21:15–17. In the journal space below, write how many times Jesus asked Peter, "Do you love me"? Then write about Jesus' response to Peter each time he answered.

Jesus forgave Peter and even told Peter to feed his lambs and sheep. "Feed my lambs" means to care for the people who believe in Jesus.

If you do something wrong and worry that God will be angry, remember this story. Tell Jesus that you love him. He will forgive you and even give you important work to do for him.

Weights and Measures

	Biblical Unit	Approximate American Equivalent	Approximate Metric Equivalent
Weights	talent (60 minas)	75 pounds	34 kilograms
	mina (50 shekels)	1 1/4 pounds	560 grams
	shekel (2 bekas)	2/5 ounce	11.5 grams
	pim (2/3 shekel)	1/4 ounce	7.8 grams
	beka (10 gerahs)	1/5 ounce	5.7 grams
	gerah	1/50 ounce	0.6 gram
	daric	1/3 ounce	8.4 grams
Length	cubit	18 inches	45 centimeters
	span	9 inches	23 centimeters
	handbreadth	3 inches	7.5 centimeters
	stadion (pl. stadia)	600 feet	183 meters
Capacity			
Dry Measure	cor [homer] (10 ephahs)	6 bushels	220 liters
	lethek (5 ephahs)	3 bushels	110 liters
	ephah (10 omers)	3/5 bushel	22 liters
	seah (1/3 ephah)	7 quarts	7.5 liters
	omer (1/10 ephah)	2 quarts	2 liters
	cab (1/18 ephah)	1 quart	1 liter
Liquid Measure	bath (1 ephah)	6 gallons	22 liters
	hin (1/6 bath)	1 gallon	3.8 liters
	log (1/72 bath)	1/3 quart	0.3 liter

The figures of the table are calculated on the basis of a shekel equaling 11.5 grams, a cubit equaling 18 inches and an ephah equaling 22 liters. The quart referred to is either a dry quart (slightly larger than a liter) or a liquid quart (slightly smaller than a liter), whichever is applicable. The ton referred to in the footnotes is the American ton of 2,000 pounds. These weights are calculated relative to the particular commodity involved. Accordingly, the same measure of capacity in the text may be converted into different weights in the footnotes.

This table is based upon the best available information, but it is not intended to be mathematically precise; like the measurement equivalents in the footnotes, it merely gives approximate amounts and distances. Weights and measures differed somewhat at various times and places in the ancient world. There is uncertainty particularly about the ephah and the bath; further discoveries may shed more light on these units of capacity.

Field Notes

Printed in the USA
CPSIA information can be obtained
at www.ICGtesting.com
JSHW040443190724
66368JS00005B/10

9 780310 455363